Achieving QTS
Assessment for Learning and Teaching in Primary Schools

20

Achieving QTS

Assessment for Learning and Teaching in Primary Schools

Mary Briggs
Angela Woodfield
Cynthia Martin
Peter Swatton

Learning Matters

First published in 2003 by Learning Matters Ltd.
Reprinted in 2004 and 2005.

British Library Cataloguing in Publication Data
A CIP record for this book is available from the British Library.

ISBN 1 903300 74 6

Cover design by Topics – The Creative Partnership
Text design by Code 5 Design Associates
Project management by Deer Park Productions
Typeset by PDQ Typesetting, Newcastle under Lyme
Printed and bound in Great Britain by Bell & Bain Ltd, Glasgow

Learning Matters Ltd
33 Southernhay East
Exeter EX1 1NX
Tel: 01392 215560
Email: info@learningmatters.co.uk
www.learningmatters.co.uk

CONTENTS

Promoting children's learning is a principal aim of schools. Assessment lies at the heart of this process. It can provide a framework in which educational objectives may be set and pupils' progress charted and expressed. It can yield a basis for planning the next steps in response to children's needs … it should be an integral part of the educational process, continually providing both 'feedback' and 'feed forward'. It therefore needs to be incorporated systematically into teaching strategies and practices at all levels.

(DES, 1988)

This book has been written for both trainees on courses to achieve Qualified Teacher Status (QTS) and Newly Qualified Teachers (NQTs) teaching in Key Stages 1 and 2 who wish to develop their understanding and practice of assessment. Assessment is not an easy area of the teaching and learning cycle. It is probably the most difficult area of any teacher's practice. The aim of this book is to give you an introduction to assessment. It will not give you a step-by-step guide for all situations, as this is not possible. This book will introduce you to different kinds of assessments and the purposes of the outcomes from these kinds of assessments. The practical tasks will offer you the opportunity to practise the different skills involved in assessing children's learning: planning, listening, asking questions, observing, interpreting, diagnosing, making judgements, conferencing and target-setting. This book will also offer you opportunities to consider the role of self-assessment in the process of assessing children's learning and setting appropriate targets for future teaching and learning. In addition it will offer you ways in which you can begin to evaluate the range and purpose of different forms of record-keeping.

No specific instrument for measuring is perfect, as you will be aware if you have ever been on a diet and tried the trick with a set of bathrooms scales – placing the scales in different locations can mean you look as if you have lost more weight than you have. If you place the scales in a location where they read as if you have gained weight, you are likely not to use that position again. Weight measured at different times of the day also appears to show fluctuating amounts of gain and/or loss. These activities lead us to question the reliability of the measurements taken. As teachers what we require is a range of potential instruments to allow us to build up as complete a picture as we can of an individual's strengths and areas to be developed. As a trainee teacher you will be in school for short periods of time on placement, and as such you will not be in the same position as the full-time class teacher who will know this class well. These teachers will also carry information about the children around in their heads, which they will not necessarily write down. Your expertise and skill in assessing and making use of the information gathered will develop with experience and depend partly on the children you teach.

The Qualifications and Curriculum Authority (QCA) has defined the key elements of assessment as follows:

Formative Assessment Teacher Assessment Assessment **for** Learning	Summative Assessment Teacher Assessment Assessment **of** Learning	Summative Assessment National Curriculum tests and tasks Assessment **of** Learning
Happens all the time in the classroom. It is rooted in self-referencing; a pupil needs to know where s/he is and understand not only where s/he wants to be but also how to 'fill the gap'. This involves both the teacher and the pupil in a process of continual review about progress. When the teachers and peers provide quality feedback, pupils are empowered to take the appropriate action. Teachers adjust their plans in response to formative assessment.	Is carried out at the end of a unit or year or key stage, or when a pupil is leaving the school, to make judgements about the pupils' performance in relation to national standards. Teacher assessment is rooted in level descriptions but is often given a numerical value. Teachers find standardisation and moderation meetings important quality assurance opportunities. Teacher assessment is a valuable part of the data held and used for management purposes.	Provide a standard 'snapshot' of attainment at the end of the key stages. A pupil's performance is described in relation to the national standards-levels. The optional tests for Years 3, 4 and 5 also provide summative assessment information for schools to use to monitor their school performance.
	Teachers often use information about children's performance in summative tests and their teacher assessments formatively.	

(Source: www.qca.org.uk/ca/5-14/afl/defintions.asp)

About this book

The focus of this book is predominantly the first of these definitions – assessment for learning and teaching. This means that the statutory assessment will be mentioned, but only briefly, as this has very specific guidance and is also subject to content changes. Statutory assessment is also one of the easiest forms of assessment to administer as the teacher has limited control over the procedures. This book tackles the more difficult area of planning for assessment, carrying out assessments and deciding what to do with the evidence collected. This links with government initiatives and guidelines on assessment, which are increasingly emphasising the way in which assessment can actually improve learning and not just attempt to measure results. This book focuses on the core curriculum of English, maths and science.

The key features of this book are the research summaries, reflection points, practical activities and web links.

- **The research summaries offer appropriate overviews of related research throughout the book, which can be followed up in more detail if required but assist you in making the links between theory and practice.**

- The reflection points at the end of the chapters are where you will be asked to consider your own experiences and target a plan for future developments. You may find these useful as part of your training course, as most courses include needs analysis and target-setting for individual students.
- There are also practical tasks for you to try out specific skills whilst you are in school. It is not intended that you carry out all these tasks but that you pick and choose the most appropriate ones based upon your experience, needs analysis, the particular placements you have and the requirements for assessment activities from your course.
- The web links and references offer you the opportunities to explore specific aspects of assessment in more detail and to keep up to date with current assessment research from the government and other professional associations.

This book will support you towards achieving the required standards for the award of QTS specifically in relation to assessment, with explicit references to the standards at the beginning of each chapter. However, a number of the tasks will also provide evidence of your achievement against other standards.

Reflection point 1

How was it for you?

Before you begin to think about assessment procedures that you will apply to other learners we want you to consider your own experiences.

Think about the following, consider the statements and write some notes against each of the statements in the table.

Statement	Yes	Maybe/ In some cases	No	Notes
1. I remember assessment at primary school.				
2. There were differences between subjects.				
3. There were differences between teachers.				
4. Assessment was mainly by weekly tests.				
5. A variety of assessment methods was used.				
6. I felt good about assessment.				

7. Assessment made me anxious.			
8. I was worried about the marks I got from assessments.			
9. Teachers' comments were very helpful.			
10. I wasn't aware of assessment until secondary school.			

The idea behind this reflection point is to get you to think about your own experiences as you develop as a reflective practitioner. You may have found that you don't remember much of your experiences at primary school and your thoughts focus more on secondary school. There are clearly some differences between assessments at these two phases of schooling. The examination system is only one. However, the point is to place yourself in the role of the learner who is assessed and receiving feedback. Even your experiences as a student at university or college would be useful to reflect upon.

At the end of this activity you will have some notes on your own experiences of assessment that you will then be asked to revisit at various points throughout this book. Experiences are likely to vary not only among individuals but also from class to class and teacher to teacher during one person's experiences. Assessment may be only associated with tests and exams in your memory, and therefore it is important to realise that as a teacher you need to have more than this narrow view of assessment strategies in order to access the information about your learners and to feed into effective teaching and learning. Reinke (1998), amongst a number of researchers who interviewed people about learning and assessment, discovered that:

> Students' assessment experiences remain with them for a lifetime and substantially affect their capacity for future learning … emotional charge is part of the character of assessment information.
>
> (Reinke, 1998)

1 GENERAL PRINCIPLES OF ASSESSMENT

Professional Standards for QTS

→ 1.6, 2.1, 2.1b, 3.1.1, 3.1.2, 3.2.1, 3.2.2, 3.2.3, 3.2.4, 3.2.6, 3.2.7, 3.3.13

Trainees must demonstrate:

- *secure knowledge and understanding of the subjects they are trained to teach, including the National Curriculum;*
- *secure knowledge and understanding of a range of monitoring and assessment strategies to evaluate children's progress towards planned learning objectives;*
- *that they know how to use assessment information to improve their own planning and teaching and give immediate feedback;*
- *their ability to assess children's progress using the relevant National Curriculum level descriptors;*
- *their ability to identify and support more able children, and those working below age-related expectations;*
- *their ability to record children's progress and achievement systematically to provide evidence of the range of work, progress and attainment over time and use this to help children review their own progress and to inform planning;*
- *their ability to use records as the basis for reporting on children's attainment and progress for children, parents and other professionals;*
- *their understanding of the contribution that support staff make to teaching and learning.*

You may find it helpful to read through the appropriate section of the Handbook that accompanies the Standards for the Award of QTS for further clarification and support.

Introduction

This chapter is designed to introduce you to the general principles of assessment and give you the necessary background information in order to begin to think about the processes of assessment as part of teaching and learning.

What do we mean by assessment? The word 'assessment' comes from the Latin 'assid-ered', meaning to sit beside (Satterley, 1989). Assessment is the process of finding out about what children can do and where there may be difficulties. At its best it provides clear information for the planning of teaching and learning, or at least for further targeted assessment. At its worst it is the process of collecting lots of data that is not used to inform individual or group needs.

Regardless of the actual methods used to assess children's learning the main aspects that are assessed are:

- **knowledge and understanding – factual information, concepts, names labels, ideas, theories, applications, connections, analogies, relationships, structures;**
- **skills – techniques, mental and physical dexterity, specific competence in particular fields, craft expertise, interpersonal skills, ability to link knowledge, understanding and skill;**
- **attitudes and values – about learning, behaviours, beliefs, subject knowledge, people, society;**
- **behaviour – social relationships, personal characteristics, competence at carrying out, fulfilling potential.**

(Wragg, 2001, p. 13)

Assessment is important, as it provides:

- **information on which to base the next teaching and learning activities;**
- **feedback for the learners to motivate them;**
- **information to assist in evaluating teaching;**
- **information that can be shared with parents and carers;**
- **information on which judgements are made about school effectiveness.**

This is not an exhaustive list at this stage but these are the areas of core importance. In order to use assessment effectively to raise standards you will need to decide how and when to assess children's attainment at the same time as planning takes place. You will need to choose appropriate techniques from a range of strategies with which you are proficient. Then, as a result of the assessments made, you will need to prepare and use manageable systems for recording the assessment outcomes. These form the aims of this first chapter.

Terminology

Assessment, like any other area, has its own vocabulary and it is important that you have a working knowledge and understanding of the terms used and how they are applied. You need to be clear about what each of the terms means before thinking about assessment in practice. The knowledge of the terminology will empower your practice as a teacher.

Practical task

Turn to the section on terminology (p. 152) and check out your understanding of the terms used in assessment practice. Note any terms with which you are unfamiliar at this stage. One strategy you could use is to allow the list to direct your reading by finding out about these terms in Chapter 1. Alternatively, you may wish to share your list of terms with tutors and/or other trainees as part of your course.

Achievement

One term not in the terminology list is 'achievement', because this is an important area to consider within the assessment process and needs consideration in greater depth. In deciding what the objectives will be for a lesson and therefore what you expect children to learn, you are making judgements about what is valued in terms of knowledge and skills. Most of these are set out for you through the National Curriculum and Strategies, which detail the expectations for children across the primary age range. The selection of the subject that is within each of the subject areas details what is valued within that subject. There are also issues about the nature of the subject being taught that needs to be acknowledged. For example, there are obvious differences between subjects like PE and mathematics in terms of the expectations of achievement and what is valued in each. You will need to consider the characteristics of the learners you are working with and how this affects what they learn and how. For example, there are clear differences in literacy skills between Key Stages 1 and 2 for children and this will affect their abilities to answer any written questions as part of the assessment process. There are other key differences between subjects which characterise progress in each subject that you will teach and assess.

Practical task

Consider what characterises two quite different subjects within the primary curriculum.

Subject	Key skills	Aspects of knowledge that are valued	What characterises progress

For example, you may have chosen art and science for this task.

Subject	Key skills	Aspects of knowledge that are valued	What characterises progress
Art	Pencil control, colour mixing	Self-expression Skills with specific techniques	More complex drawings, use of different mediums for images.
Science	Fair testing, investigative processes	Evidence-based judgements	Hypothesis setting, awareness of the elements of fair testing, increased knowledge and understanding.

How do you get started?

Getting starting with assessment can appear quite daunting, but it is important to start with what is feasible and not try to do too much.

Ideally the cycle of planning, teaching and assessing actually starts with assessing the learners' needs. However, most of the planning you are doing is likely to start with planning some teaching before using the assessments of the children and evaluation of the teaching to plan the next steps in teaching and learning. Assessment must be planned at the same time as teaching and learning.

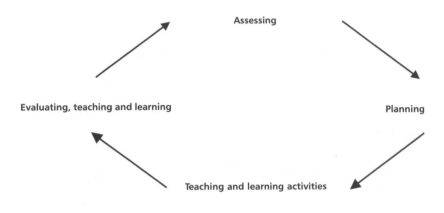

Figure 1.1

Effective formative assessment as above is a key factor in raising children's standards of achievement. QCA describes the key features of assessment for learning as involving the use of classroom assessment to improve learning. Central to formative assessment, or assessment for learning, is that it:

- **is embedded in the teaching and learning process of which it is an essential part (as shown above);**
- **involves sharing learning objectives with pupils;**
- **helps pupils to know and to recognise the standards to aim for;**
- **involves pupils in self-assessment;**
- **provides feedback which leads pupils to identify what they should do next to improve;**
- **has a commitment and confidence that every pupil can improve;**
- **involves both the teacher and the pupils reviewing and reflecting on pupils' performance and progress.**

(Adapted from www.qca.org.uk/ca/5-14/afl/ and Neesom, A, 2000)

Planning for assessment

In order to plan for assessment you will need to consider what information you want to collect and why. This is likely to vary with subject within the curriculum and with the number of learners you are trying to assess. This section will look at a range of strategies that you could plan for. The following section will explore some of the ways of carrying this out in the classroom.

QCA gives some very clear guidance in the form of a checklist for finding evidence of the use of assessment for learning. The planning section of this guidance is useful to consider at this point. Evidence can be found in plans with:

- **emphasis on learning intentions and sharing them with pupils and other adults in the classroom;**
- **assessment criteria for feedback and marking, self and peer assessments;**
- **differentiated groups, changes to differentiated grouping;**
- **review time and flexibility built in;**
- **annotations with notes of pupils to focus on because they need additional/ consolidation activities;**
- **use of guided group sessions for explicit formative assessment opportunities;**
- **adjustments highlighted/crossed out – what did/did not work and why;**
- **good questions recorded that really reached pupils' understanding/ misconceptions;**
- **events that showed unexpected outcomes.**

(Source: www.qca.org.uk/5-14/afl/checklist.asp)

This is quite a daunting list but you will find as your planning develops that you can find evidence of all of these elements across a number of plans. It will not be appropriate to expect to have all of these in all of your plans. The key issue here is that in order to assess effectively you need to build opportunities into your planning so it becomes an integral part of your planning and thinking about teaching and learning.

The other area to consider, when planning assessments, relates to the recent work in schools focusing on creativity and learning styles. This work acknowledges that children have preferred learning styles which are, in turn, related to the ideas of 'multiple intelligences' – interpersonal, intrapersonal, bodily/kinaesthetic, logical/ mathematical, verbal linguistic, musical, visual/spatial and naturalist. As a result of this work, schools are acknowledging that offering children opportunities to record their learning from a specific lesson might give a choice based on these intelligence areas. In being offered these opportunities children are more likely to show you the true range of their learning rather than a narrow part of their knowledge.

The role of your own subject knowledge

When planning teaching and learning you will need to identify the key concepts, facts, skills and attitudes appropriate for the subject. This is one point where your own subject knowledge is important. You need to know the connections between facts that will promote progress in children's understanding rather than create problems that will lead to misconceptions. Will you be able to identify the key issues for a specific area that you will teach? Will you notice the errors/misconceptions? Can you see errors in spelling patterns?

Practical task

For the next science lesson you teach try your own concept map for this topic. What connections are you making? Check out the connections with the appropriate literature on the area. Did you miss any key connections? If not, well done – now you will be moving on to select the appropriate learning objectives for the lesson and/or sequence of lessons.

From objective to method of evidence collection

First, when planning a lesson for any subject you will have to set objectives for the lesson and expectations of not just the amount of work that you want children to complete but more importantly what you want them to learn. Having set these objectives for the first lesson in a sequence you will assess the children's learning against these objectives. It is therefore important that you set appropriate and achievable objectives for all children in the class even if you have different levels of expectation to cater for owing to the differentiation within the class. For example:

At the end of the lesson most children will have...
Some children will have...
A few, or perhaps a specific group of higher ability children, will have...

When you write the objectives you should do so in such a way that you can find evidence of children achieving the learning expected and where the teaching is focused. They will be more specific showing what you will be looking for in terms of a learning outcome. For example, children will give examples of known facts of doubles and explain how they will use these to derive near-doubles. Children will demonstrate they can use full stops and capital letters in the right places. These need to be clearly defined and written in such a way that you will be able to collect evidence of whether or not children have achieved the objectives set. As an example of this, an objective could be stated as 'children will be able to describe the features of a river', or 'children will be able to explain orally their methods of calculating using short division'. If you state the objectives in terms of what children will know or understand, how will you be able to collect evidence of knowledge and or understanding? When writing objectives the following words could be used to phrase an objective in order to make it easier for you to collect evidence of achievement: 'state...describe...give examples... suggest reasons... explain... evaluate... pick out... distinguish between... analyse... carry out... summarise... show diagrammatically... compare... demonstrate...'. This is not an extensive list, but it does give you some examples.

When you have decided on the learning objectives that you are going to assess during your lesson you will want to look at how you might collect the evidence in order to make the appropriate judgements. The following is a list of ways in which you might collect that evidence. What is important is that the methods of collection match the activities given to the children, their age and ability. You should also not try to use a wide variety of methods within one lesson. Examples include:

- observation of a child/group working (see page 18 for details);
- questioning (see page 21 for further details);
- child-to-child discussion: children's discussion can provide useful insights into their thinking. This can be planned as listening time or recorded using a tape recorder;
- child-to-teacher discussion – this is linked to questioning but may also be an in-depth discussion outside the teaching time;
- concept mapping – individual (see page 12 for further details) or group;
- before and after ideas – this is similar to concept mapping but you will not be looking for the links in the same detail but rather the ideas themselves;
- matching of key concepts with definitions to show understanding – this can be a specific task, which requires children to use certain knowledge in order to match concepts with definitions;
- reports written – a written account of the child's work;
- reports oral – individual or group;
- oral presentations – individual or group;
- demonstration through peer teaching, which needs to be set up carefully with a clear focus – unless the children are very confident it is best to start in small groups;
- tape recordings (see discussions);
- drawings;
- labelled diagrams;
- graphs;
- models;
- storyboards;
- zigzag books;
- cartoon strips;
- drama;
- games, e.g. true/false;
- multiple choice questions;
- problem solving questions;
- peer assessment (see page 28 for further details);
- small books on specific topics;
- brochures;
- completed writing frames;
- photographs;
- equipment used on a table top and left for assessment, e.g. sorting of materials, numbers, types of story;
- computer print-outs;
- completion of worksheet;
- completion of written work;
- role-play;
- quizzes;
- and last but not least, tests!

Concept mapping

An alternative way of findings out about children's understanding is to use a technique more often associated with science teaching, and that is to ask children to construct a concept map. These can range from simple labelled diagrams and drawings to more complex maps, which involve asking children how they connect a wider range of words. Arrows can be added to show the direction of the relationship between items.

The following are simple examples of this technique from science.

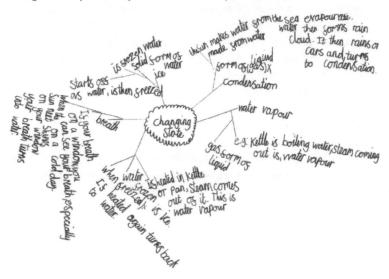

Figure 1.2: Year 5 changing state map.

You would need to know the context and prior experience of the children to know whether or not they are making connections from what they have been taught or new connections by themselves.

RESEARCH SUMMARY

Concept mapping has been used by Baroody and Bartels (2001) to investigate assessment of understanding in mathematics. They argue that because understanding can be viewed as the connections between two pieces of information, a concept map is one way to access children's understanding of mathematics. They looked at the number of concepts and examples linked together in the concept maps drawn, suggesting that the more detail and the greater the number of linking concepts the more complete and flexible the child's understanding. They suggest the following are the advantages of using concept mapping in assessment:

1. *Concept mapping can be used for diagnosis and instructional feedback as well as grading.*
2. *With concept mapping, assessment can be an integral aspect of teaching and vice versa.*
3. *Concept mapping can be used to assess group work as well as individual progress.*
4. *Concept mapping provides a rich alternative to traditional written tests and contributes to using multiple means of assessment.*

(Adapted from Baroody and Bartels, 2001)

Practical task

Decide upon an area of the curriculum and get a group or class of children to produce concept maps for a specific area. Try this before and after teaching that topic to see the differences in the children's thinking about the area.

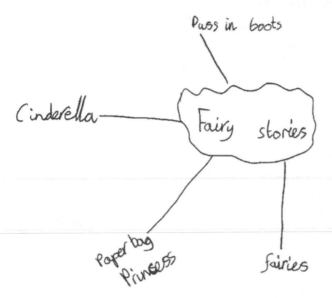

Figure 1.3: A concept map produced before teaching the topic.

Figure 1.4: A concept map produced after teaching the topic.

The examples here are from an English topic – an area of the curriculum not usually associated with concept mapping. Between the 'before' and 'after' you can see an increase in the ideas associated with fairy stories. In the 'after' map you can see how the child has started to put some of the ideas from specific stories together.

Using other adults in assessing children

Increasingly schools are making use of more classroom assistants, and as part of your planning you will need to consider how to use these additional adults in the classroom. The starting point for making this decision as a trainee is the class teacher that you will be working with – he or she will know the classroom assistants and their specific skills. A discussion with the class teacher will enable you to find out the most effective way to use the support and to tailor what you expect of the adults to match their skills and experience.

There are three kinds of support the classroom assistants may need – information, instructions and subject knowledge. For examples of practical tasks that include instructions and information it is worth looking at Additional Literacy Strategy (ALS), Further Literacy Strategy (FLS) or the mathematics Booster materials. Coupled with this is the issue of the classroom assistant's subject knowledge and whether there is a need to support their knowledge so they can support the children during their activity. This last area is a very difficult one, as you will not have time to build up the kind of relationship necessary to explore this in depth and you will need to rely upon the class teacher's knowledge of the classroom assistant for your planning. Some schools have specific policies outlining the precise roles and responsibilities of classroom assistants, whereas others may have a less structured approach to their use. Assistants will need some guidance to work with an individual and/or a group. At the same time as working with the group they are in a good position to observe responses and behaviours first-hand. This can provide you with another pair of eyes and ears to inform the totality of your assessment strategy. Other adults may notice different responses and behaviours from children in a small group rather than the whole class. This information can feed into the overall assessment of individuals and the planning for the next lessons. Other things that you could ask the teaching assistant to do might include:

- **prompting shy or reticent children;**
- **signing or translating vocabulary, phrases, questions or requests;**
- **helping children to use specific resources including Information and Communication Techology (ICT);**
- **ensuring that children can interpret instructions correctly, concentrate and behave responsibility;**
- **reminding children of key teaching points from earlier in the lesson;**
- **encouraging participation;**
- **scribing for an individual.**

Many adults you will work with in schools are experienced and highly skilled, and will use their initiative inactivities that you have planned for them to use with children. However in order that you appear professional and show that you have considered their role, a dialogue and written guidance can be helpful in establishing a good working relationship with other adults. As part of your planning you will need to share the overall plan for the lesson. Most additional adults have limited time outside the lesson to discuss plans and activities in detail. One way is for you to prepare a summary specifically focused on the group that you have planned that they work with, such as the one that follows.

Classroom Guidance and Assessment Sheet

Name of teacher:	Class/set:
Date:	Lesson focus: Subject and ICT if appropriate
Name of classroom assistant/additional adult:	
Brief details of the activity and the nature of the support required:	
Key questions to ask when the children are working on the activity:	
Subject and ICT specific vocabulary to use:	
ICT resources to be used:	
Key issues/operating instructions for using ICT resources:	
Subject learning objectives:	ICT objectives where appropriate:
1	1
2	2
3	3

Assessment sheet for the assisting adult to complete.

Children	Can do			Difficulties			Next steps in support
	1			1			
	2			2			
	3			3			
	1			1			
	2			2			
	3			3			
	1			1			
	2			2			
	3			3			
	1			1			
	2			2			
	3			3			
	1			1			
	2			2			
	3			3			

Practical task

Plan a lesson using another adult to work in the classroom with you. Try out the sheet above, or use a similar approach in discussion with your class teacher and the classroom assistant if possible. Arrange a time for you to evaluate this approach with the adult and amend your planning accordingly.

The way you will be able to use additional adult support in the classroom will depend upon previously established roles for assistants in schools, as mentioned before but it will also be an area you will develop as part of your practice. The current standards include a specific reference to the use of additional adults to support teaching and learning, and clearly assessment is an integral part of that process. Care needs to be taken that you don't ask classroom assistants to take on roles outside their experience and confidence without discussion and support. But, by the same token, their skills and experience can be undervalued. Discussion with all parties involved is crucial to develop the use of classroom assistants effectively, especially in relation to assessment.

Target-setting

Setting targets makes you focus on what children are actually learning, not what you think you are teaching.

(OFSTED/DfEE, 1996)

Target-setting at different levels is part of the planning process. Targets are specific learning objectives focusing on different groups for a variety of purposes but all working towards progression in learning and improving standards. They can be at school, class, group and individual level. At school level the targets are set on the basis of National Test results. Here we are concentrating on the target-setting that is identified through assessment and planned into the teaching and learning in daily lessons. This might result in having a target board on the classroom wall with the class targets for the week or similar period. These targets would be discussed as part of the ongoing work in the class and act as an aide-memoire for all children. This looks like a dartboard in some classrooms in order to draw the children's eyes towards the items displayed. Use a capital letter at the beginning of every target sentence.

Figure 1.5: A dartboard-style target for display in the classroom.

At an individual and class/group level, target-setting should also take account of any targets set out in Individual Education Plans (IEPs) for children with special educational needs and the education plans for looked-after children (see page 31 for further details on both these categories of children).

RESEARCH SUMMARY

The Gillingham Partnership Project was significant in establishing ways forward for target-setting that focused on developing children's writing.

It seems clear that individual writing targets for some children both motivate and give a clear focus for achievement. However, a number of factors need to be balanced when deciding whether to introduce individual targets wholesale.

- *Setting matched targets is the first hurdle, best done in conference with the child and with some kind of target prompts. These often need to be broken down and quantified (specific examples and number need to be spelled out).*

- *Keeping track of the subsequent progress is probably the most difficult organisational feature and works best when children are encouraged to keep a tally of how many times they have achieved their target.*
- *The clearer and better quantified the individual target, the easier it is for a child to recognise their achievement.*

Ways in which teachers appear to have had the most success have been as follows:

- *investing a lot of time at the outset in negotiation with each child to explain and decide his or her first target, setting the scene for the whole focus;*
- *making sure the target is crystal clear and matches the child's ability;*
- *getting children to tally each time they believe they have achieved their target;*
- *making flaps, cards or other devices visible and easy to handle;*
- *making sure the child knows how to go about meeting the target;*
- *making sure there will be opportunities for the child to cover and therefore achieve the target, or, at least, saying when it is unnecessary to refer to the target.*

(Clarke and McCallum 2001(b))

Practical task

Choose a subject for which to make a target board. Identify some common targets for the class and display them ahead of the lesson. At the start of the lesson draw the children's attention to the targets – for example, when writing what they are aiming for. At the end of the lesson, again use the targets to discuss how the activities have progressed and evaluate the use of the board.

Assessment during the lesson

During the main activity or activity times in a lesson you could be working with a group and choose to assess specific skills, knowledge and/or understanding of the topic taught. One trainee achieved this by developing her own sheet on which she recorded the information to assist her in future planning. This kind of assessment needs to be considered as part of the planning process, ensuring that the other children in the class are engaged with appropriate tasks so that you will be able to assess a small group in more detail. If you don't consider this as part of the planning process you will not be able to spend time with a group.

Consider the following issues as you plan to assess a small group as part of the lesson:

- **What are the skills, knowledge and abilities I want to assess?**
- **Are there specific difficulties I want to focus on?**
- **Is this group a quiet group where I don't know the children well?**
- **Which three or four specific things do I want to assess?**
- **How long will this take me? Plan in small amounts of time with this group at different stages in the task whilst remembering to monitor the rest of the class in terms of behaviour and activity.**

Date:	Observer:	Group:

Context:

Objective(s):

Notes:

Objective(s) achieved:

Targets:

Review:

Observing children while they work is a key skill of teaching. Most of the time you will asked by tutors and school-based staff to be aware of what is going on all around the classroom at all times, so that you notice if a child makes a dash for the door or a disagreement starts between children. This is quite a different observational skill from that needed when assessing children. You cannot follow everything, as it is possible to become distracted by other events and therefore to be making judgements about a child's achievements on partial information.

Observation is really the only method of assessing much of the work children will do in the classroom. It is a good method of collecting information about a child or group of children across a range of issues. The downside of using observation is that it can require a concentrated and narrow focus in order to really see what is going on. You have probably been asked on one of your placements to observe a child closely when you haven't been teaching. You will have seen from this how much information you can gain from this process, but also how time-consuming it was to carry out. As a result you will also be aware that it requires support and focused planning of other adults in the classroom in order to allow you to concentrate on your observation. This is not the best method to use for a one-off assessment as you may find that, having selected the focus for your observation, the children do not respond in ways that allow you to make clear judgements about a chosen area.

Practical task

Plan a lesson where you will focus on a small group for teaching and assessing. Use the format above to record your observations. Afterwards, consider:

- if you need to re-design the proforma for future observations;
- any planning issues that arose, which will help you be a better observer in future lessons, e.g. did you allow enough time in order to observe in detail? Were you able to monitor the rest of the class at the same time?

Planning time for an assessment conference with an individual child

Individual conferences with children can tell you a lot about their understanding, achievements and possible difficulties, so planning time for this kind of in-depth assessment is an important part of the planning stage. As a trainee you may be able to carry out this kind of task in your non-contact time. When teaching full-time, when would you be able to undertake such a task?

Practical task

Plan to spend ten minutes with a child to talk about his or her work in a particular subject, review progress and together set targets for the next few weeks' work. In setting targets you need to choose ones that are achievable both in quality and in content. Concentrate on one area at a time so the child doesn't feel swamped. Always pick out things the child has achieved as well so the conference doesn't dwell on negative issues alone – praise success. Remember this process is not just for special educational needs (SEN) children but for all children. Target-setting can be a good way of raising expectations for the higher-attaining children. Set a time by which you will review these targets. The main purpose of this conferencing and target-setting is to give children some goals to aim for against which they can measure their own success. It may be possible for some children to conference in small groups but there will be children for whom it is better to work on an individual basis.

You will need to keep a record of targets set. An example follows.

Child's name:	Year:
Term:	Class:
Date of assessment:	Date of review:
Targets set:	Comment on achievement:
1. 2. 3.	

The format above is quite formal and the kind of record that a teacher might keep. Below is a more child-friendly format that could be decorated further to make it more personal and used with children as part of their role in assessing and target-setting.

Child's name:	Year:
Date:	Class:
I can:	I need help with .... or These are my targets for the next half term ....
1. 2. 3.	1. 2. 3.

Questioning children in order to assess their achievements

It can sound easy to ask children questions so you can assess their knowledge and understanding, but it takes careful planning to be effective. Questioning pupils is a key teaching strategy in the National Numeracy Strategy, for example.

It can be used to:

- **assess children's understanding;**
- **assess errors and misconceptions;**
- **understand the thinking behind children's methods;**
- **focus discussion by using children's ideas;**

- **elicit concrete examples or principles or concepts;**
- **explore language and vocabulary;**
- **encourage reflection.**

There are two main types of questions that you will use in teaching – closed and open. Closed questions usually require one-word or brief responses, whereas open questions require more extensive responses.

There are different times in lessons when you will want to use these types of questions. When you are keeping the pace brisk, most of your questions are likely to be closed, and you won't want extended explanations from children. The questions are likely to be of the following form:

- **How many?**
- **How much?**
- **What would … ?**
- **What are … ?**
- **What is … ?**

At other times within the same lesson you will want to find out more about children's understanding and to use their ideas to focus discussion on concepts. The questions are likely to be in the following form:

- **How did you work that out?**
- **How did you decide to work it out that way?**
- **What does this mean and can you give me an example?**
- **Can you explain how you did that?**
- **How did you decide what would happen next in the story?**
- **Where did you look for information in order to answer the questions?**

These questions require extended responses and offer the opportunity for in-depth discussion of knowledge and understanding that closed questions do not. Brown and Wragg (1993) describe the common errors in questioning:

- **asking too many questions;**
- **asking a question and answering it yourself;**
- **asking questions only of the brightest or most likeable;**
- **asking a really difficult question too early;**
- **asking irrelevant questions;**
- **asking the same types of questions;**
- **asking questions in a threatening way;**
- **not indicating a change in the type of question;**
- **not using probing questions;**
- **not giving children the time to think;**
- **not correcting wrong answers;**
- **failing to see the implications of answers;**
- **failing to build on answers.**

(Brown and Wragg, 1993, p. 18)

'It all depends on the question you ask' is an account of research by Khwaja and Saxton (2001) focusing on the questions asked of primary children to assess their scientific knowledge and understanding. This research specifically looked at what children know about the human skeleton. The researchers found that if asked to draw what they thought was inside their bodies, children' responded differently according to their age. Young children mentioned bones more frequently than older children. Khwaja and Saxton suggest two possible reasons for this. First, that when asked to draw what they think is inside their bodies children may simply draw the organs and parts that are of most interest to them. Or, that as they learn more about the digestive and respiratory system these elements feature more in their drawings than do the bones. As a result of their work Khwaja and Saxton suggest that the task given to children to assess what they know and understand must allow them to demonstrate the full extent of that knowledge and understanding. They do not offer an alternative question for children to answer, but you may like to try this question with some children to see what responses you gain. Then think about how you might rephrase the question in order to gain a more detailed insight into the children's knowledge and understanding.

Listening

Associated closely with questioning is the skill of listening. You may be very good at asking open questions but miss part of the children's responses. You can often pick up information in order to focus questions to specific children/groups to check out understanding. There are two ways of listening. You can become more aware of the children's discussion when working and pick up on issues arising from the discussions, or you can set up work that facilitates discussion to which you plan to listen.

HOW TO LISTEN
Before you start:

- **decide upon a focus;**
- **plan the lesson so that you have time to listen.**

During the lesson:

- **concentrate;**
- **take notes, or use a tape recorder.**

After the lesson:

- **use the notes and recordings to make judgements, focus additional questions and add to your records.**

The advantages of this are many.

- **Although you need to concentrate, you can allot yourself a set time and collect a considerable amount of information.**
- **It can allow you to refer to specific events and conversations when you talk to individual children, e.g. in a conference with a child.**
- **You may hear things by chance as well, which can prove helpful in improving your understanding of children's thinking.**

There are also disadvantages.

- It can be tempting to interrupt – think before you speak. If you note issues you can follow them up later rather than stopping the discussion.
- It can be hard to concentrate, depending upon what else is going on in the classroom.
- You will need to guard against premature or inaccurate interpretation. If you are unsure check with the individuals concerned.

(Adapted from Clemson and Clemson 1991, pp. 53–54)

Practical task

Plan to listen to a group working on a task and record what you are listening to on a proforma such as the following:

Date:	Listener:	Group:
Context: Objective(s):		

Children's names	Notes on what was said during the activity and by whom:

Comments:

After the lesson:

What has been achieved?

Targets – in terms of future questions for individuals:

     – in terms of future learning:

Planning for children's self-assessment

In order that children know what is expected, the teaching and learning plan needs to identify clearly the learning objectives for each lesson. These remain the close focus during the teaching if the learning objectives are explicitly shared with the children in language that is accessible and age-appropriate. It is worth explicitly acknowledging this in your planning as a reminder that you need to do this at appropriate points in the lesson. There may be transition points in mathematics or English that require sharing different learning objectives for different parts of the literacy and numeracy lessons, for example. The other issue from the 'learning to learn' research is planning in opportunities to review the children's work and what they have learnt. This is part of the do, review, learn and apply cycle that has emerged from the initial stages of this research. This is a research project over a number of years so not all of the findings have been published at this stage. The key issue overall is making the learning accessible and explicit to children and allowing space for them to review their learning at different points during a lesson, not just at the end.

Practical task

Review your planning, especially your learning objectives.
Ask yourself the following questions:

1. *Are there appropriate learning objectives?*
2. *Are the learning objectives written in appropriate age-related 'child speak' so they can be shared with the children?*
3. *Have I identified specific points when I will share the learning objectives with the children?*
4. *Have I also planned to share any specific assessment criteria, which is linked to the learning objectives?*
5. *Is it clear what the purpose is of any activity and why children are being asked to complete the task?*
6. *Are there spaces for review for the children? Are there opportunities to record their thoughts about their learning in different ways?*

If the answers to these questions are all 'yes', then you have a plan in which you are giving the children access to your expectations for learning. If you have answered 'no' anywhere, then you have to think carefully about how easy it will be for children to know what you are expecting of them during the lesson.

QCA has suggested that teachers need to consider the following if they are to improve learning through assessment:

- **Explain clearly the reasons for the lesson or activity, in terms of the learning objectives.**
- **Share the specific assessment criteria with the children.**
- **Provide effective feedback to the children.**
- **Involve children in their own learning.**

- Help the children to understand what they have done well and what they need to develop.
- Show the children how to use the assessment criteria to assess their own learning.
- Adjust teaching to take account of the results of assessment.
- Recognise the profound influence that assessment has on the motivation and self-esteem of children, both of which are crucial influences on learning.

(Adapted from: www.qca.org.uk/ca/5-14/afl/involving_pupils.asp)

For science, Goldsworthy (2000) suggests looking at 'Fantastic Feedback' and suggests that teachers should share an understanding of the learning objectives with the children. This helps the teacher and the children to focus on the task. She suggests the following as guiding principles for identifying, sharing and assessment against the learning objectives:

Fantastic feedback means: share learning objectives.
Fantastic feedback means: move the children's thoughts forward.
Fantastic feedback means: challenge misconceptions.
Fantastic feedback means: create an ethos of trust.

Guidance for children about self-assessment

The list above from QCA appears straightforward but the last point about children using assessment criteria to assess their own learning is actually quite difficult. If someone asks you how well you think you are doing on your course at the moment, what would you say? Would you dwell on the things that are not going as well as you'd like? Would you gloss over the difficult areas? How would you know what the questioner wanted in the absence of any guidance? And you have some experience of self-assessment! The fact is that it is inappropriate and ineffective to ask anyone to carry out self-assessment without some guidance. The kind of guidance you provide will depend upon the age of the children, the subject of the lesson and the key learning objectives for the activity/lesson. All primary age groups are capable of self-assessment but you will notice that with increased age children can assess in more depth. Young children can acknowledge that they have done well but they are often influenced by adults' comments about their work, merit marks or having got everything right. They are able to discuss what they like but find articulating why they like things more difficult. In Key Stage 2 they are capable of clearly stating their own opinions about their work, though some children will still be heavily influenced by their teacher's comments.

If you want to give some guidance in order to help children look for important elements in their work you could offer a checklist (Wragg, 2001). The focus here is not to evaluate the whole task but to allow children to check their work before handing it in for marking, for example. The requirements should be brief and require a yes/no or a tick answer – this would be mainly for use with Key Stage 2 children. Verbal instructions could be given to a group of Key Stage 1 children focusing on similar items before they hand their work in order to encourage them to take ownership of their work.

What are you looking for:	Tick/cross
1. Have you written the date and title?	
2. Have you given three reasons why you liked the story?	
3. Have you written your answers in sentences?	
4. Have you written an alternative ending to the story?	

You may feel that some items are more about presentation than learning, but it provides a starting point for discussion depending upon the objectives for the lesson and the criteria shared with the class for the assessment of a finished piece.

The following is one example of prompt questions from the Gillingham Partnership Project, focusing on teachers' and children's use of formative assessment in the classroom. These questions have been trailed in classrooms during the project. Again, these examples are clearly more appropriate for Key Stage 2 than Key Stage 1. With Key Stage 1 you might choose to focus on a much smaller number of items and to ask them as oral questions rather than give them out on a worksheet. Sharing answers to two questions during a lesson will support the development of the children's assessment skills. Be prepared, though, as the younger children will also want to know what you think and may actually ask you directly. If you are in a Key Stage 1 class try asking a specific question, for example, 'How do you remember how to write the word "the"?' By focusing on a specific issue you are drawing out the potential learning strategies but also finding out about how the children felt about learning. 'It is easy to remember – I can see the word in my mind before I write it down', or 'I have practised the word over and over again'. You may find a range of responses. What is important is allowing children a secure space to say what they think – there are no wrong answers.

Self-evaluation: thinking about what happens when we are learning

- **What did you find easy about learning to … ?**
- **What are you most pleased with about learning to … ?**
- **What really made you think/did you find difficult while you were learning to … ?**
- **What helped you when something got tricky about learning to … ?**
- **What could you do to help yourself understand better?**
- **What do you need more help with about learning to … ?**
- **How would you do things differently next time now you know what you know now?**
- **What can you do now that you couldn't do before?**
- **What have you learnt that is new about … ?**
- **How do you think we can use what we've learnt today and in the future?**
- **How would you change this activity for another group/class who were learning to … ?**

Choose one or two, add words of learning intention each time and stick to wording given here carefully.

(Clarke, 2001(b))

The first part of the Gillingham Partnership Project focused on communicating learning intentions, developing success criteria and children's self-evaluation. Here we are specifically looking at the self-evaluation part of this project. This research shows that if children are to be encouraged to develop effective self-evaluation then several aspects need to be considered by the teacher.

- *Children need to be given prompts, either orally or in writing to assist self-evaluation (see above for an example).*
- *There needs to be discussion about what appropriate responses to evaluation questions might be.*
- *Allowing children to work in pairs on evaluation questions gives more chance for children to articulate their views.*
- *Stopping in the middle of a lesson to allow space for self-evaluation is a useful strategy so that children don't see evaluation as something that only occurs at the end of the lesson.*
- *Aiming specific questions at certain children can assist the discussion.*
- *Evaluation is not effective when it is seen as just going through the motions, i.e. 'ritualising sessions'.*

(Clarke, McCallum and Lopez-Charles, 2001)

As a teacher you can involve children in self-assessment and develop their skills in this area by:

- **making the learning purpose of the activity clear to the child – why they are being asked to do the task;**
- **making it clear what it is the audience will be looking for in the piece of work;**
- **involving children in discussion about their learning;**
- **talking to children about what they feel they need in order to work well;**
- **helping the children to judge the quality of their work in terms of process and understanding as well as presentation;**
- **helping the children to identify their own strengths and weaknesses and encouraging them to take steps to meet these needs;**
- **encouraging children to realise that their satisfaction with their work is important and 'pleasing themselves' is more important than pleasing the teacher;**
- **helping them to recognise positive and negative aspects of their work in order to set achievable targets and incorporate review strategies.**

Peer assessment

Perhaps your image of peer assessment is children swapping their work and then the teacher reading out the answers and the children marking each other's work, often much more rigorously than the teacher might. There are other conceptions of peer assessment. These require children to be guided and/or trained in order to make effective use of the process of assessing others' work and receiving feedback from their peers. Children require guidance about what to look for, starting on a small scale. For example, with a piece of writing, the children need guidance about what to look for in a story beginning. Does the start of the story make you want to read on? Then try to get children to articulate exactly why they have said yes or no. Choosing children who you know will be able to express themselves clearly allows for peer modelling of a 'good' answer for the whole class without putting others on the spot at the early stage of working with this strategy of assessment. The same issues discussed in relation to key stage and self-assessment applies to peer assessment. Children need to feel comfortable with self-assessment before they can work on peer assessment.

RESEARCH SUMMARY

Lindsay and Clarke (2001) discuss examples of involving children in self- and peer assessment to enhance primary science. The work was based in a junior school in Years 5 and 6 in Tower Hamlets in London, and specifically looked at lessons working around Attainment Target 1: Considering and evaluating evidence, and Attainment Target 3: Materials – thermal insulation. After the lessons the children were asked to self-mark. They were then asked to underline the three areas in which they believed they had achieved the learning intention most effectively, and to make a wavy underlining to identify an area they considered needed addressing. Some children were encouraged to pair up and mark each other's work. Children's assessment of their peers gave the teachers a valuable insight into the children's own understanding of skills and knowledge. In the lessons' plenary some self-evaluation prompts were offered to draw things together. As a result of this work the following advantages of using these strategies have been identified.

- *Children take ownership of their learning.*
- *The teacher has the opportunity to focus on one group.*
- *Children see assessment as a process in which they are involved and to which they can make a contribution.*
- *Children have control over their learning and see themselves as partners in the teaching–learning process, raising their self-esteem.*
- *Teachers gain greater insight into the children's assessment of self and peers.*
- *Children can use the skills of self-marking in a variety of contexts and develop greater perseverance with learning, as they are more involved in and have greater control over outcomes.*
- *Self-marking can clarify ideas for children, helping them to refine and question their own concepts.*
- *Children become more self-critical and pro-active as learners.*
- *Children focus upon the next goal in their learning. They feel they are setting the next target rather than it being externally imposed.*
- *Children become more scientific in their enquiries, as self-assessment encourages them to be constantly involved in the scientific process and their role within it. Through the self-assessment children raise questions and this opens up new avenues for investigation.*
- *Children are aware, through paired-marking, that they are communicating to an audience and therefore writing/reporting is a purpose.*

(Adapted from Lindsay and Clarke, 2001)

What is feasible?

We have now looked at a range of strategies that you can employ in the classroom. We have highlighted the need for planning in order that you can carry out focused effective assessment. When you have chosen your assessment strategy and planned that into your lesson you will need to carry this out. What is important is not to try to cover too much in one go, as this will not give you the depth of information to make accurate judgements relating to attainment and progress.

You have been introduced to a range of methods and assessment tests – you might try just one of those in a given situation. Part of the purpose of your time in school is to try out these strategies, including tests, in order to decide which is the most appropriate in a given situation. This will depend upon the children, their range of abilities and your developing skills as an assessor. You might try targeting assessment at different points in a topic or different points in a lesson, or at different groups.

Tests

Tests are the most familiar method of assessment. We have introduced you to a range of other methods to use in school but there may be times when you want to give a short 'test' at the end of a topic or towards the end of a placement in school. Tests are not inherently bad things, but they require more planning than most people imagine. First, look at what you want to assess. What is the content? No test should ask something of the learner that has not been part of the teaching and learning (content validity). What notice and guidance will you give your class? Will you need additional adults? (See the next section on diversity of children's needs.) How will you mark the test? What feedback will you give the children? What form will the test take – written, multiple choice, or something, else? Maybe a mixture of formats?

Practical task

For a topic you have taught, design and carry out a test with some of the children. As you mark their work and offer feedback, answer the following questions.

- *Does the test give you sufficient information in order to make a secure judgement about attainment and progress?*
- *Were there questions that all the children found difficult? Why? How would you change this in future?*
- *Were all the children able to complete the test?*
- *What additional information do you need in order to make secure judgements for all children?*
- *Were there any issues about the administration of the test?*
- *What were the children's reactions to a test situation?*
- *Were there any other issues you noticed?*

Dealing with the diversity of children's needs in assessment

Most classes will include children with a range of abilities and this is still true of 'sets' though the range may be slightly narrower in top groups. When carrying out assessment you will need to be aware of the difficulties that some children may encounter in this situation. In this next short section, the following areas are introduced in order to develop your awareness of the range of needs associated with assessment. These are:

- anxiety;
- gender;

- special educational needs (SEN);
- looked-after children;
- English as an additional language (EAL);
- more able children;
- the potential for bias in your judgements.

Anxiety

You may be one of a large group of adult learners who suffer from anxiety in any assessment situations. Children can suffer the same anxieties. Try where possible to make any assessment situation a natural part of the teaching and learning process. Emphasise the need to 'try your best' and reassure children that they do know the answers to questions because they have been working on those areas. You may also wish to give some tips about reading questions and making sure the children answer the question asked. It is surprising how many children don't actually do this, because they panic or forget. Some children can feel under a lot of pressure to do well, so don't forget that anxiety doesn't just affect those who might have difficulties.

Gender and achievement

In the 1970s and 1980s there were concerns about girls' achievements in mathematics and science in particular. More recently, concern has focused on boys' achievements in English.

RESEARCH SUMMARY

The Department for Education and Skills (DfES) funded a three-year project, running from June 2000 to December 2003, entitled Raising Boys' Achievement (ref: www.rba.educ.cam.ac.uk). This has been a research and intervention project based at Cambridge University Faculty of Education. The project has sought to identify the strategies that schools have employed to raise educational standards for boys (and girls), the processes by which this has been achieved, and the extent to which any improvements in performance have been sustained over time. At the time of writing the project has not yet been completed, so final results are not available. However, certain issues are emerging, including the findings that:

- *in relation to assessment boys appear to favour short-term targets;*
- *building self-esteem is important in raising achievement;*
- *identifying conditions under which boys feel they perform best in school and building upon this is key.*

Special educational needs (SEN)

The National Numeracy Strategy (NNS) and the National Literacy Strategy (NLS) both provide guidance for teaching children with SEN, which you will find helpful in teaching and assessing children. When you have planned your assessment strategy for the class you will need to consider how you can enable SEN children to show you what they know to the best of their abilities. This may mean any of the following:

- an adult reading questions for a child or group;
- taped questions for a child to listen to;

- additional resources to support children, e.g. a table square for an autistic child who has difficulty remembering known facts, or a spell checker for a dyslexic child;
- large print work for children with sight difficulties;
- alternative ways of recording responses;
- asking children to complete a given assessment task in smaller periods to assist attention;
- accepting that for some children with behavioural difficulties this may not be the best time to push for completion of the task given.

Looked-after children

This is a label that covers a wide range of children and their needs. It can include children who are in temporary care and therefore may be new to the school and will need time to settle. A child in care or foster care may also have SEN, though this can be a generalisation that is overused. Identification of the child's needs in his or her 'education plan' will help you to see what exactly the needs may be in terms of assessment.

English as an additional language (EAL)

Children who have English as an additional language may need picture clues on assessment tasks, simplified language or a mother-tongue reader.

More able children

Children are not all of the same ability – this is a very obvious statement, but it needs consideration when you may have more able or gifted children in your class. As part of assessing their specific needs it would be worth considering whether or not they need to complete the same tasks as the rest of the class. They may start at a different point, or have a more investigative task to explore their thinking skills more fully. For very able children between the ages of 9 and 13 there are world-class tests available for mathematics and problem-solving. These tests have been trialled in the UK, Australia, New Zealand and the United States. More details can be found on www.worldclassarena.org/v5/default.htm – this site gives details of online tests available and for whom they would be most suitable.

In general, any assessment practice should acknowledge the full range of learning styles and competencies in order to allow children to show specific attainment in any curriculum subject. Formative assessment can be particularly useful for more able children who are often quick to act on feedback. This can enable them to reflect on their own learning, increasing autonomy and independence. Assessment strategies should allow challenges for the more able which are appropriate to their abilities, and assessment tasks will need to be differentiated appropriately. These children are also affected by praise and need as much motivation as others. More able children benefit from a mixture of teacher and peer assessment in order to articulate and analyse learning outcomes, strengthening the understanding of the individual and groups. Identifying the criteria in the work of others can help more able children to enhance their understanding of the learning process and the subject matter.

Language, context and relevance

The language used in some commercially produced assessment tasks/sheets may not be the same as the language you have used in your teaching. The language should match. Sometimes in an effort to make assessment questions relevant to children, the questions are set in a 'real-life' context. This can cause confusion if the children are not familiar with the context or items used in the questions. For example, in the Key Stage 2 mathematics test C level 6 paper in 2000 there was a question about making shortcrust pastry that included the ingredients flour, margarine and lard. Many people do not now use lard and therefore children might have been concerned that they didn't understand the whole question, as they didn't know what one of the ingredients actually was.

RESEARCH SUMMARY

Cooper and Dunne (2000) have researched the National Tests (National Curriculum Tests) questions for mathematics at Key Stages 2 and 3. They focused on the fact that some of the questions used in the tests produced unintended difficulties for children because of the ways mathematical operations were embedded in textually represented 'realistic' contexts. Difficulties in understanding the rules of the game could be the reason why some groups of children performed poorly on this type of question. In test questions with 'realistic' elements children are required to draw upon their everyday experiences as well as their previous knowledge and understanding of mathematics. At the end of Key Stage 2, working-class and intermediate-class children perform less well than service-class children on 'realistic' items and the effect is large enough to make a considerable difference to children's futures. Differences between genders are similar though smaller. Cooper and Dunne's research suggests that as teachers we need to be aware of the predisposition and effects of prior knowledge of our children when they respond to test items that have 'realistic' elements.

Practical task

Review your assessment items in your teaching files. Do they allow access for all children? How could you alter items to allow access? Try writing a couple of assessment questions. Rephrase them to cater for specific groups of children. If you have the opportunity, try your chosen questions out on children. Can they read the questions? What do they think the question is asking them? This will assist you if you have children with specific needs in your class.

Acknowledging your own bias

When you are making judgements about the attainment and progress of any child, you need to be aware that your judgements may be affected by bias. This bias could come from your previous knowledge of the child, how they have been categorised by yourself or others, and/or your relationship with the child. So much of the 'art of teaching' is about personalities that it is hardly surprising that the relationships between the learner and the assessor are of crucial importance. Children are very sensitive to these relationships but so are adult learners. You may remember the teachers at school you tried to do well for because you liked them and so liked what they taught. You may have also experienced similar feelings in your learning after school. If you feel that you may be influenced by your attitudes to a child use another person, such as a teaching assistant or other teacher, to pick up additional information about the individual in order to come to a balanced judgement. It is important that you are secure in the judgements you make as they can affect a child's self-esteem as well as influencing future opportunities (for example, setting).

Assessment of children when using ICT as part of their learning

When using ICT to support the teaching and learning of any subject you must be aware of how ICT can change the task given. In terms of assessment you need to be clear about the difference between ICT learning objectives and subject-related objectives supported by ICT. A child's competence with ICT may be very good, but this may not necessarily correspond at the same level to attainment within the subject.

Assessment after the lesson

After the lesson you will review the learning that has taken place during the lesson and use this information to plan the next stage of learning. This should be completed as soon as possible after the lesson. The focus is the children's learning. Here you will want to note those children who did not achieve the objectives for the lesson and to try to note why you think they had difficulties or specific errors and misconceptions that did not allow them to achieve. You will also want to know if children have exceeded your expectations and specifically what they demonstrated in terms of their understanding during the lesson which could be used to take them further. This will be part of your assessment evidence that you will later transfer to records of progress and attainment.

Lesson evaluations

Pupils not reaching objectives	Pupils exceeding the objectives
Notes for next day/week focusing on teaching	
Good aspects	Areas for development

As you make a judgement about children's learning against the objectives, the following flow charts may assist you by focusing your attention on the precise nature of the objectives and the steps that are necessary in the children's learning in order to achieve the planned learning. You will need to map out the potential progression expected so you can identify difficulties that can be rectified in the next lesson. To show you how this might work, the first chart is set up for a mathematics lesson.

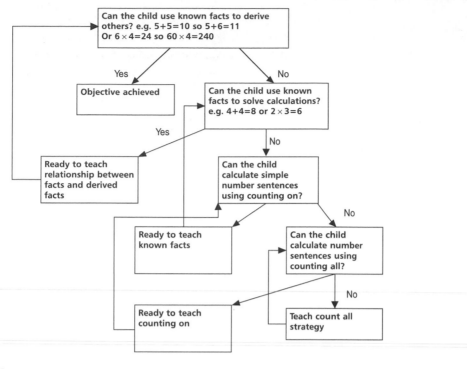

Figure I.6: Assessment flowchart starting with using known facts to derive others.

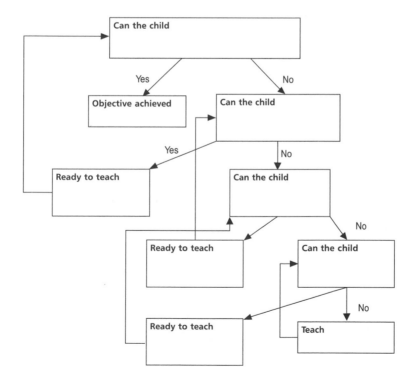

Figure I.7: Assessment flowchart starting with the key objective for the lesson.

Practical task

Using the blank flowchart, fill in the steps you have identified for a specific objective within a lesson. Try to match where you think the children within a group are on the flowchart during and/or after the lesson. Evaluate this method of assessment. Would you use this again? For a specific lesson, or subject? What changes would you make?

Marking children's work

Regular marking should inform the teacher of pupils' progress, stimulate dialogue about the work and encourage pupils to improve. However these powerful potential benefits of marking are only sometimes realised.

(OFSTED, 1998, p. 92)

Providing feedback to children about their work/responses is an essential part of assessment for learning, and one focus of that feedback is marking. Schools often have clear policies on marking, or at least guidance in relation to the style of marking. It is worth asking your class teacher/mentor about your placement school's views about this issue. The following section focuses on some general issues about marking for you to consider alongside school-specific guidance. The feedback focus has shifted as QCA describes it (2002), from telling children what they have done wrong to children being encouraged to reflect on their own work and what they need to do to improve, and discussing this with the teacher. Therefore giving feedback involves making time to talk to children and to teach them how to reflect on both the learning objectives and their work/responses.

Try to mark the following children's work. As you do so, think about what you can tell from each piece of work.

A

This is a Year I child's written work.

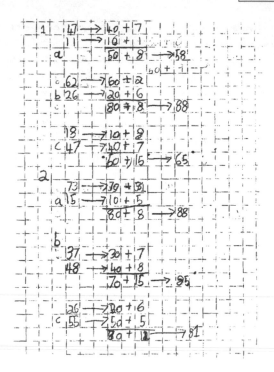

B

This is a Year 4 child's mathematics work.

At this stage we have not provided specific comments about these examples of children's work. You would need to know what the learning objectives were for the lesson and the context of the work before you could make specific judgements. The idea is to get you to think about what kinds of assumption you are making about the work as you mark. You may have decided that some issues need addressing just by looking at the work.

The following offers some guidance about good practice in marking.

- **Before children are asked to hand in work they should know that you will be marking this specific task, rather than it being self-marked or peer-marked.**
- **Children should be encouraged to reflect upon how well they have achieved the learning objectives.**
- **Children should also be encouraged to reflect on the quality of their work/ responses and how they might improve them. Children need guidance on this if they have not undertaken this kind of task before. They may require prompts/ questions – examples of these can be seen in the self-assessment section. This is also not something you would ask children to complete at length for each piece of work and it might be completed orally as you mark, not just in writing.**
- **Children should know what you will be focusing on when marking and it should relate to individual targets set where appropriate. Some schools have adopted the WILF acronym of 'What I Look For' in each piece of work so all children know what is expected of them.**

- Children should have been reminded about any layout or presentation issues before submitting any work, not afterwards.
- If children have achieved the key objective of the lesson, then they need to be told that they have in the feedback to celebrate the achievements made.
- Likewise if they have not achieved the objective then they need to know what to do in order to achieve the objective.
- Acknowledging progress is very important, particularly for children who have not fully achieved the objective.
- When receiving the work you will want to look for successes as well as aspects that need to be developed in order to form some future targets for the individual. You are therefore building upon the successes, not just looking at areas of weakness.
- Indicate which answers are correct and which are not. (Make sure you get it right!) Do not mark a whole page of work wrong – see this child separately. Make sure that you indicate if there are any corrections to be completed and why.
- Try to write comments that inform the child and that are in legible handwriting. Avoid writing 'good' or 'well done' on their own – say why a piece of work is good.
- Set children between one and three targets as a result of marking this piece of work.
- Set yourself specific areas that you wish to record about a particular piece of work. For example, the following table is one approach to marking science written work.

Child	Number of metals tested	Number of non-metals tested	Examples of children's responses	Examples of marker's comments

(Evans, 2001)

- Choose a colour pen that is in contrast to the child's work – there may be a school policy about not using red.
- If you are not sure what is going on when you look at a child's work, do not mark it. Instead, set aside time to talk to the child individually. We can make assumptions about difficulties based upon the recording that we see, and that can lead us to plan intervention that is not appropriate.
- Marking can assist you as a teacher in collecting evidence of children's progress and attainment. You can use this as formative assessment, which will inform the next stage of planning.
- Marking will give you and others an indication of the amount of help needed to complete a task, if this information is added to your comments on the work – for example, 'Robert worked with James on this problem', or 'Amy used a

calculator for this work', or 'Rumma and Ambia worked on this piece of text collaboratively'. You can use this as the basis of child conferences and to assist you in compiling summative reports for parents. The following table will help you think about the type of feedback that you give when marking.

	Type A	Type B	Type C	Type D	
Positive feedback	Approving	Rewarding	Specifying attainment	Constructing achievement	Achievement feedback
	Rewards	Positive personal expression; warm expression of feeling; general praises; positive non-verbal feedback	Specific acknowledge-ment of attainment/use of criteria in relation to work/behaviour; teacher models; more specific praise	Mutual articulation of achievement; additional use of emerging criteria; child role in presentation; praise integral to description	
Negative feedback	Punishing	Disapproving	Specifying improvement	Constructing the way forward	Improvement feedback
	Punishing	Negative personal expression; reprimands; negative generalisations; negative non-verbal feedback	Correction of errors; more practice given; training in self-checking	Mutual critical appraisal	

(Adapted from Gipps, 1997, cited in Conner, C. (ed.), 1999)

QCA (2002) has identified the characteristics of effective feedback from research on the LEARN Project and other commissioned work.

- Feedback is more effective if it focuses on the task, is given regularly and while still relevant.
- Feedback is most effective when it confirms the children are on the right tracks and when it stimulates the correction of errors or improvement of a piece of work.
- Suggestions for improvement should act as 'scaffolding', i.e. children should be given as much help as they need to use their knowledge. They should not be given the complete solutions as soon as they get stuck – they must think things through for themselves.
- Children should be helped to find alternative solutions if simply repeating an explanation leads to failure.
- Feedback on progress over a number of attempts is more effective than feedback on performance treated in isolation.
- The quality of the dialogue in feedback is important and most research indicates that oral feedback is more effective than written feedback.
- Children need to have the skills to ask for help and the ethos of the school should encourage them to do so.

(Source: www.qca.org.uk/ca/5-14/afl/)

RESEARCH SUMMARY

The LEARN Project (Bristol University, 2000) focused on learners' expectations of assessment requirements. The project interviewed over 200 students of different ages (Year 3 to Year 13) in a range of schools to gain insights into their perceptions of assessments they undertake and how assessment is used to help them improve their work and learning. Fifty-six of these students were identified as low achievers within their class or set. The students' responses give a partial view of their motivation, their problems and successes with learning and assessment, and what types of feedback helped them improve their work. The main findings were as follows.

Low-achieving students:

- *showed motivation that was highly dependent on context, on liking the teacher and on the subject;*
- *tended to be concerned with 'performance' rather than 'understanding', and a few had an attitude of 'learned helplessness';*
- *demonstrated poorer understanding of assessment requirements than their peers;*
- *revealed an understanding of what to do for individual tasks that was inconsistent – sometimes they could explain tasks clearly, while at other times they struggled;*
- *had little understanding of how tasks fitted into the 'big picture' of the course;*
- *were very dependent on teacher-set standards when judging the quality of their work;*
- *rarely reported having opportunities to develop self-assessment skills;*
- *were often confused by effort and attainment grades;*
- *sometimes felt that their effort was not recognised by teachers;*
- *preferred feedback that was prompt and delivered orally;*
- *were often unable to use feedback effectively;*
- *felt that feedback that was constructively critical helped improve their performance.*

(adapted from: www.qca.org.uk/5-14/afl/involving.pupils.asp)

As part of the marking and feedback process you can model the quality expected by showing children the learning strategies and goals. Often the language of assessment can be confusing for young children. By sharing other children's completed work you can begin to construct a shared understanding of the quality of learning outcomes. Children can use the work of others to develop their reflective and analytical skills, which they can then transfer to self-assessment of their own work. The work needs to be unnamed in order that children do not make comments about someone's work on the basis of the person.

Practical task

Collect some pieces of work showing a range of learning outcomes for a class. Arrange a swap with another trainee with a similar-aged class to try out the idea of children looking at other children's work. It is important that you provide the learning objectives for the lesson and a little context for the children and the fellow trainee who will be looking at the work. You may find it useful as a pair of trainees to discuss the key points from this task and reflect upon how you could build upon this as part of your assessment strategy.

QCA (2002) suggests that sharing work can offer the following opportunities.

- encouraging pupils to listen to the range of pupils' responses to questions;
- showing pupils the learning strategies;
- showing pupils how the assessment criteria have been met in some examples of work from children not known to the pupils;
- encouraging pupils to review examples from anonymous pupils that do not meet the assessment criteria, in order to suggest the next steps to meeting the assessment criteria;
- using examples of work from other pupils in the class to highlight the ways they meet the criteria or standards.

(Adapted from: www.qca.org.uk/ca/5-14/afl/modelling_quality.asp)

RESEARCH SUMMARY

Shirley Clarke was invited to set up an evaluation project of formative assessment strategies used in the teaching and learning of writing in the Gillingham Partnership schools, based on the practical strategies continually developed with teachers (Clarke, 1998 and 2001). The strategies are based, in particular, on the significant findings of Black and Wiliam (1998), which indicated that formative assessment raises children's attainment, increases their self-esteem, gives them a greater stake in their learning and enables a greater prospect of 'lifelong learning'. One interesting aspect of this research was that children demonstrated their natural desire to focus on improvement rather than the more negative correction, and they revealed, thorough interviews, remarkable perception about their roles as learners in the feedback process. Another was the locus of control of the assessment process with the strategy presented to teachers as a 'way in' to focused feedback, with control placed firmly in their hands. Within this research there was observed the beginning of the continuum in which control gradually shifts from teacher to child.

Involving children immediately in analysing their own work resulted in disappointing outcomes. Without models of improvement suggestions and solutions, children simply guess at what they might do or say. Without clear learning intentions, they focus on surface features of their work.

Marking against very focused learning intentions was found by teachers to be more manageable, and children could more easily identify and understand their successes and improvements. This in turn provided motivation for the children, and resulted in children writing at a relatively higher standard when making improvements as soon as they were allowed to work on the feedback given. In this way the feedback 'scaffolded' future learning. There were some difficulties with giving continuous oral feedback as teachers felt an urge to comment on everything. They found themselves getting side-tracked by other achievements. They believed that certain aspects, like handwriting, needed constant comment (Clarke, 1998 and 2001).

POTENTIAL PROBLEMS

In trying to give children effective feedback you need to be aware of potential problems you may encounter in giving the feedback yourself and/or trying to interpret the feedback from others.

- There is a tendency for teachers to assess the quantity of work completed and the quality of the presentation rather than the quality of learning (this can be seen in the earlier research summaries and from student folklore of lecturers weighing assignments to in order to arrive at a grade).
- There is a tendency to give greater attention to marking and grading, and this has the knock-on effect of lowering children's self-esteem rather than providing focused advice for improving learning.
- There is a tendency to compare children with each other, which results in demoralising the apparently less able children.
- There is a tendency for teacher's feedback to serve social and managerial purposes rather than to focus on learning (an example of this might include comments like 'you could have written more if you had not been talking so much' or 'this is not enough work for a whole lesson').
- Feedback cannot be focused on improving learning if teachers do not know enough about the children's needs.
- Feedback cannot be focused on improving learning if teachers do not have sufficient subject knowledge to be able to identify the key issues relating to the subject and how specific misconceptions can affect/impact upon future learning.

How do you judge good models of recording assessment outcomes?

Keeping meaningful records sounds quite easy, yet it is a difficult aspect of assessment. It is possible to keep records for classes of children that may be clear and precise and easily interprete, but they will only show you which areas of the curriculum children have 'covered'. This means that the children will have had access to those particular parts of the curriculum that are indicated in the records.

These can be highlighted items on a list of the objectives/topics that are planned for a specific period, like a half-term or term, or they can be part of the records against the objectives showing those children who were present for that lesson. The following is part of this type of record.

Name	Attendance register															Objectives achieved								
	✓ = present O = absent															1	2	3	4	5	6	7	8	9

This kind of record is important for teachers to show what they have taught and to ensure a broad and balanced curriculum for all. It enables targeting children who have been away for specific lessons/topics to ensure equality of opportunity.

You will encounter a number of different models for record-keeping that are used in different subject areas. How do you judge if they are good models? One way to look at this issue is to study some examples and evaluate how useful you would find them if given them at the beginning of a placement to assist you in planning for the range of ability in a class.

The example below is taken from part of a class record and shows the key objectives from the Numeracy Strategy. It is for a class of Year 5 children.

Key Objectives Year 5	Sue	Bill	Sue	Raminder	Mark	Simon	Judy
Multiply and divide any positive integer up to 10 000 by 10 or 100 and understand the effect	/	∧	—	∧	/	/	—
Order a given set of positive and negative integers	/	/	/	/	/	/	/
Relate fractions to division							
Use decimal notation for tenths and hundredths	∧	∧	Δ	∧	∧	∧	Δ
Round a number with one or two decimal places to the nearest integer							
Relate fractions to their decimal representations							
Calculate mentally a difference such as 8006–2993	Δ	Δ	Δ	Δ	Δ	Δ	Δ

The teacher has used a sequence of triangle-forming symbols, where / indicates that an objective has been introduced, ∧ indicates that the objective has been partially met and Δ indicates the objective met. The symbol ⎵ indicates that the objective has been met fully and consolidated.

Practical task

What interpretation would you make of the record above? Remember this is only a small part of the record for these children, though you still would be able to make some judgements about what is going on here.

You may have considered that gaps indicate that those areas have not been taught. There appears to be a difference in achievement, particularly with the first objective. This could give you an indication of the groupings needed in teaching this area again and an indication of the range of differentiation required. The differences between the categories assigned are difficult to be precise about without further information but this kind of record can provide a starting point. It is useful to discuss your interpretation of a similar record with the class teacher who has made these judgements. Usually the whole school will work on what each category means so there is a shared understanding of when to use which category. This is something you may not have an opportunity to be part of during your school placements.

You may come across records that use a 'traffic lights' approach. This is where items are highlighted with green if they have been achieved, orange (amber) if more work is needed on the objective and red if the objective has not been achieved at all. It is possible to refine the categories, adding notes where it is useful and appropriate but not for all children. So for the record sheet shown earlier the following coding could be added:

Name	Attendance register												Objectives achieved								
													Date	Date	Date	Date	Date	Date	Date	Date	Date
	✓ = present O = absent												1	2	3	4	5	6	7	8	9

A = achieved, HD = had difficulties with, NA = needs attention, U = unfinished

Objective 1:

Objective 2:

The dating of records like this can assist you in showing progress over a period of time. It may also highlight if any children have difficulties with retaining information, which could affect their achievement.

The following is a sheet that could be attached to the class record identifying specific issues that require attention for individuals and/or small groups of children.

Assessment for the needs attention category
Name: Subject: Date:
Objective:
Difficulties (errors, misconceptions, other problems):
What is required to rectify difficulties?
Evaluation of intervention:

What do you do with assessment outcomes?

The following will be the results of your analysis of children's learning:

- **Identify and celebrate children's achievements.**
- **Identify errors and misconceptions to be rectified in the next lesson.**
- **Re-group children according to their achievement and enable easier targeted teaching.**
- **Identify children for whom you do not have sufficient evidence to make a secure judgement. Further investigation must be planned in order that a judgement can be made as accurately as possible.**
- **Identify issues to be addressed in your teaching of specific facts, skills and knowledge in order that children's learning can progress.**
- **Identify individuals/groups to target with support of additional adults.**
- **Provide evidence for identification of SEN, more able and EAL children.**
- **Provide evidence to support and discuss attainment and progress with parents/ carers/children.**
- **Identify individual/group/class targets.**

Working in partnership with parents/carers

One key use of assessment outcomes and records is in dialogue with parents and carers. This can be in the form of an oral or written report of an individual child's attainment and progress. Oral reports usually take place at parent–teacher consultations during the year. These usually include an opportunity for parents/carers to look at their children's work and then discuss issues arising. This also includes sharing the child's current individual targets. It can be quite a stressful experience for all parties. You may have an opportunity to sit in on consultations during one of your placements, though clearly parents would have a choice about whether or not you are observing or participating. If you are involved as a trainee then you need to have some notes about each child available to support your discussion, as everyone finds it hard to remember everything when in a potentially stressful situation. You may also find it helpful to note the key issues that you want the parents to know about – both strengths and areas for development. Be prepared for questions from some parents. Some of these can appear quite challenging but more often they come from a real concern about their child's achievements. Some examples of questions you might get are:

- **What level is my child working at in … ?**
- **How come s/he can do these at home but appears to be getting these all wrong at school?**
- **Could s/he have more homework in … ?**
- **Why isn't my child reading these books?**
- **Why is my child in this group?**
- **Can they have spelling tests/tables?**
- **How will they do in the National Tests?**
- **And (sometimes people are looking this far ahead), are they university material?**

This appears quite a negative list, and it is these kinds of questions that will cause the most problems. Of course there are always positive aspects of the discussion on these occasions, but they are much easier to deal with than difficult questions like the ones above.

Practical task

Find out about parent–teacher consultations during your next school placement. What are the arrangements for these events? If you are to be involved, prepare some notes and discuss these with an experienced teacher.

When writing reports you need to remember who the audience is and what they expect to read about their child. Written reports should be supportive and meaningful (e.g. not full of education jargon). They should include positive remarks, but they should not hide any difficulties. They should include the areas that have been studied by the child as well as achievements, and aspects of knowledge, skills, understanding and application. Make sure that it is clear which subject you are writing about and that the comments are not so general that they could be about any subject.

Sometimes it is appropriate to mention presentation and/or attention to tasks by some children. It can also be appropriate to mention other aspects of behaviour if they affect a child's learning. All reports should include some indication of strengths and of the targets for each subject.

All children must have a report on their learning each year from Year 1 to Year 6 in primary schools and all must include information about attendance at school during the year. Although it is not compulsory to have written reports for Reception children, many schools do so. Schools must provide an opportunity to discuss the Reception baseline assessment. At the end of each key stage (Years 2 and 6), the report must include copies of the National Test results for the individual child, for the school and the national comparisons. The latter can be problematic in terms of interpretation, made as the national results are most often from the year before rather than from the current year, owing to timing and availability of results.

On the following pages is an example of a child's report from Year 2, which includes the child's own contributions as well as information about National Tests and the curriculum for the year.

Reports can come in different formats. They can be computerised and generated from a bank of suggested phrases, tick sheets, full written reports or any combination of these. Computerisation can lead to quite impersonal reports though it can save time. Written reports usually include targets for the next term/year. They are also usually written when the teacher has had the class for a considerable part of the year and therefore knows the children well.

Changes have been made to the requirements for keeping reports.

- **Copies of all children's reports will form part of the child's educational record.**
- **All parents have the right to see their child's records.**
- **All children have the right to see their records. This is no longer related to the age of the child. Instead, children who submit written requests to see their records should be allowed to do so unless it is obvious that they do not understand what they are asking for.**
- **Schools should not disclose anything on children's records which would be likely to cause serious harm to the child's physical or mental health or that of anyone else – including anything which suggests that they are, or have been, either the subject of or at risk of child abuse.**

(DfEE, 2000)

Practical task

Find out about the format of written reports on your next school placement. What are the similarities and differences between the previous example and the format you have been given from your school? With the support of an experienced class teacher write a draft report for a child in the class you are teaching. Discuss the language used and how you might share the information with the child.

English:

Speaking and Listening Ellen joins in discussions confidently and her contributions show that she listens carefully to others.

Reading Ellen enjoys books and stories and her understanding is excellent. She is able to explain what she likes or dislikes about books, can comment on the behaviour of characters and use information books to answer questions. She finds the mechanics of reading difficult but uses all the strategies she has been taught and is making good progress. She must continue to read widely at home and at school.

Writing The content and structure of Ellen's writing is excellent. She chooses words and expressions carefully to create interesting stories. She uses the main features of different forms of writing appropriately. Spelling is difficult for Ellen but she listens well, spells familiar words correctly and tries hard to use the phonics she has been taught. Well done Ellen!

Mathematics: Ellen enjoys mathematics, works hard and has achieved well for her age. She handles numbers to 100 confidently and can explain her methods and reasoning when solving problems. She needs now to extend her multiplication and division skills.

Science: Ellen enjoys science and her attainment is above average for her age. She has good ideas for investigations. Ellen is able to make predictions and suggest reasons for the things she observes. She records her results clearly and systematically. Well done Ellen!

History: Seaside holidays were the focus of our first history topic. We used photographs, artefacts and books to compare and contrast holidays in the past and holidays now. We have also studied Florence Nightingale and her work and learnt about the Great Fire of London.

Ellen contributes well to discussions. She uses artefacts and historical evidence appropriately to support her comments. Well done Ellen!

Geography: Our seaside topic provided opportunities to use maps, books and travel brochures to compare Long Itchington and a seaside locality. We identified places on UK and World maps and thought about the similarities and differences in the environments. We very much enjoyed sharing our work in a class assembly.

Ellen has made thoughtful and sensitive comparisons between environments. She has made some very good maps and plans. Well done!

Technology: The children enjoyed learning about wheels and axles and using them in their model making, but our favourite project has been about puppet making. The children designed, made and evaluated glove puppets based on characters from traditional stories. They made patterns, cut out felt and stitched fabrics before adding features. The project culminated in puppet shows performed in a class assembly and thoroughly enjoyed by both pupils and parents.

Ellen has good ideas, plans carefully and works skilfully. She makes thoughtful evaluations and has produced some excellent work.

Art: Work in art has included drawing from observation and imagination, exploring colour and texture and developing designs. As part of their work on the seaside the children made careful drawings of natural objects then chose one of the drawings to develop into a design for a shell collage.

Ellen explores materials and ideas confidently. She produced a very pleasing shell collage and was able to explain what she liked and disliked about her work. Lovely work Ellen - well done!

Music: During the year the children have contrasted high and low sounds using the voice and instruments. They have explored ways in which sounds are made and have responded to symbols to create their own sound sequences. They particularly enjoyed singing songs about the seaside when learning about rhythm patterns.

Ellen enjoys music and always works with enthusiasm. She listens well and makes excellent contributions to our lessons.

PE: The children have experienced a wide range of gymnastic, dance and game activities to help improve and extend their skills. They have learnt how to use apparatus correctly and safely and co-operated with other children in partner and small group work. They have learnt about the effect of exercise on their bodies and the importance of physical activity to their general fitness and health.

Ellen enjoys PE and has worked hard and successfully in all areas. I have been particularly pleased with her work in dance.

ICT: The children have been taught the ICT skills needed to create, correct and save a picture using "Splosh" and have demonstrated their ability by producing pictures of shells. They have used "Textease" to word process class stories, individual sentences and an anthology of favourite poems. Work in literacy and numeracy has been supported by "Learning Ladder" and they have used ICT to produce graphs in science and maths.

Ellen works confidently and has enjoyed using a word processor to support her writing.

RE: During our RE lessons we have been finding out about some of the stories, celebrations, festivals and customs associated with Christian and Islamic traditions. We have visited Holy Trinity Church and the Congregational Church. Our "Christening" provided an excellent opportunity for the children to understand the meaning of the service before enjoying a celebration tea.

Ellen always listens well and takes an active role in our discussions. She is sensitive to the ideas of others.

General comments:
(Including Personal Social & Health Education)

Ellen has an excellent attitude to all areas of school life. She listens well and tries hard to put into practice the things she has been taught. She is a very keen, enthusiastic and hardworking member of the class and deserves to do well. She is keen to please and responds well to praise and encouragement. Keep up the good work Ellen!

Headteacher's comments: *Another excellent year for Ellen. Her enthusiasm is a joy and it is no surprise that she had made such good progress again. Well done Ellen. Thank you for being such a hardworking girl.*

Class teacher's signature: **Headteacher's signature:**

July 02.

End of Key Stage 1 Assessment Results 2002

Name: Ellen
Pupil Number:

Date of Birth:
Reg. Group: 22

ENGLISH

Teacher Assessment Results

Speaking and Listening	Level 3
Reading	Level 2
Writing	Level 2

Task and Test Results

Reading Task	Level 2C
Reading Comprehension Test	Level 2B
Writing Task	Level 2A
Spelling Test	Level 2

MATHEMATICS

Teacher Assessment Result

Level 2

Task or Test Result

Level 2A

SCIENCE
Teacher Assessment Result

Level 3

There are no tests or tasks in Science for Key Stage 1.

Level 1 and W (meaning working towards Level 1) represent achievement below the nationally expected standard for most 7-year-olds.
Level 2 is divided into three grades - 2A, 2B and 2C. Level 2B represents achievement at the nationally expected standard for most 7-year-olds. Children who achieve level 2C may not be progressing well enough to achieve level 4 when they are 11.
Levels 3 and 4+ represent achievement above the nationally expected standard for most 7-year-olds.

School no:

Comparative Report:

SUMMARY OF THE NATIONAL CURRICULUM ASSESSMENT RESULTS OF PUPILS IN THE SCHOOL (2002) AND NATIONALLY (2001) AT THE END OF KEY STAGE 1, as a % of those eligible for assessment.

TEACHER ASSESSMENT: Percentage at each level

		Dis.	Abs.	W	1	2	3	4+
ENGLISH TA	School	0	0	4	4	68	24	0
	National	0	0	3	12	64	21	0
Speaking and Listening	School	0	0	0	8	68	24	0
	National	0	0	2	11	63	24	0
Reading	School	0	0	4	0	68	28	0
	National	0	0	3	13	55	29	0
Writing	School	0	0	4	8	68	20	0
	National	0	0	4	12	71	12	0
MATHEMATICS TA	School	0	0	0	4	84	12	0
	National	0	0	2	9	63	26	0
Using and Applying Mathematics	School	0	0	4	16	44	36	0
	National	0	0	2	13	62	22	0
Number and Algebra	School	0	0	0	4	84	12	0
	National	0	0	2	9	63	26	0
Shape, Space and Measures	School	0	0	0	16	40	44	0
	National	0	0	2	11	64	24	0
SCIENCE TA	School	0	0	0	4	60	36	0
	National	0	0	1	9	65	24	0
Scientific Enquiry	School	0	0	0	12	56	32	0
	National	0	0	2	12	65	21	0
Life Processes and Living Things	School	0	0	0	0	48	52	0
	National	0	0	1	7	63	28	0
Materials and their Properties	School	0	0	0	4	48	48	0
	National	0	0	1	8	65	25	0
Physical Processes	School	0	0	0	4	64	32	0
	National	0	0	2	10	65	23	0

TASK AND TEST RESULTS: Percentage at each level

		Dis.	Abs.	W	L	1	2	2C	2B	2A	3	4+
Reading Task/Test	School	0	0	4		0	68	16	36	16		
	National	0	0	3		13	55	15	21	19		
Reading Comprehension Test	School	0	0		0		68	20	28	20	28	0
	National	0	0		2		53	13	20	20	29	0
Writing Task/Test	School	0	0	4		12	72	16	32	24	12	0
	National	0	0	5		9	76	27	30	19	9	0
Spelling Test	School	0	0		4		60				24	
	National	0	0		11		52				23	
Mathematics Task/Test	School	0	0	0		4	56	8	20	28	40	0
	National	0	0	2		7	62	15	24	23	28	0

Dis. = excepted or disapplied under sections 364 or 365 of the Education Act 1996
Abs. = absent from the Tasks/Tests
W = working towards level 1
L = below level 2 threshold for the Reading test and/or Spelling test when required to be entered for the test

School no:

Ellen 22 - Registration Certificate

Wk	Wk Begin	M.T.W.T.F.	Poss	Act	Percent	Unauth	Analysis	
02	03/09/01	XXXX/\/\/\	6	6	100.00	0	Attendances	: 348
03	10/09/01	/\/\/\/\/\	10	10	100.00	0	Authorised Absences	: 0
04	17/09/01	/\/\/\/\/\	10	10	100.00	0	Unauthorised Absences	: 0
05	24/09/01	/\/\/\/\/\	10	10	100.00	0	Missing Marks	: 0
06	01/10/01	/\/\/\/\/\	10	10	100.00	0	Possible Attendances	: 348
07	08/10/01	/\/\/\/\/\	10	10	100.00	0		
08	15/10/01	/\/\/\/\/\	10	10	100.00	0	% Attendances	: 100.00
09	22/10/01	##########	0	0	0.00	0		
10	29/10/01	XX/\/\/\/\	8	8	100.00	0	Approved Educ. Activity: 0	
11	05/11/01	/\/\/\/\/\	10	10	100.00	0	Lates Before Reg Closed: 0	
12	12/11/01	/\/\/\/\/\	10	10	100.00	0	Lates After Reg Closed : 0	
13	19/11/01	/\/\/\/\/\	10	10	100.00	0	Unexplained Absences : 0	
14	26/11/01	/\/\/\/\/\	10	10	100.00	0		
15	03/12/01	/\/\/\/\/\	10	10	100.00	0	Key to Codes	
16	10/12/01	/\/\/\/\/\	10	10	100.00	0	------------	
17	17/12/01	/\/\/\/\/\	10	10	100.00	0	/\ Present	
18	24/12/01	##########	0	0	0.00	0	! No Attendance Required	
19	31/12/01	##########	0	0	0.00	0	# Holiday for all	
20	07/01/02	XX/\/\/\/\	8	8	100.00	0	* Not on roll	
21	14/01/02	/\/\/\/\/\	10	10	100.00	0	- All should attend	
22	21/01/02	/\/\/\/\\XX	8	8	100.00	0	@ Late (after reg closed)	
23	28/01/02	/\/\/\/\/\	10	10	100.00	0	B Educated off site	
24	04/02/02	/\/\/\/\/\	10	10	100.00	0	C Other authorised circumstances	
25	11/02/02	##########	0	0	0.00	0	E Excluded	
26	18/02/02	/\/\/\/\/\	10	10	100.00	0	H Annual family holiday (agreed)	
27	25/02/02	/\/\/\/\/\	10	10	100.00	0	I Attending interview	
28	04/03/02	/\/\/\/\/\	10	10	100.00	0	L Late (before reg closed)	
29	11/03/02	/\/\/\/\/\	10	10	100.00	0	M Medical/Dental	
30	18/03/02	/\/\/\/\/\	10	10	100.00	0	N No reason yet provided for abs	
31	25/03/02	##########	0	0	0.00	0	O Unauthorised circumstances	
32	01/04/02	##########	0	0	0.00	0	P Approved sporting activity	
33	08/04/02	/\/\/\/\/\	10	10	100.00	0	R Religious observance	
34	15/04/02	/\/\/\/\/\	10	10	100.00	0	S Study leave	
35	22/04/02	/\/\/\/\/\	10	10	100.00	0	T Traveller absence	
36	29/04/02	/\/\/\/\/\	10	10	100.00	0	V Educational visit	
37	06/05/02	##/\/\/\/\	8	8	100.00	0	W Work experience	
38	13/05/02	/\/\/\/\/\	10	10	100.00	0	X Only staff should attend	
39	20/05/02	/\/\/\/\/\	10	10	100.00	0	Y Enforced closure	
40	27/05/02	/\/\/\/\/\	10	10	100.00	0	Z Not part of school's year	
41	03/06/02	##########	0	0	0.00	0		
42	10/06/02	/\/\/\/\/\	10	10	100.00	0		
43	17/06/02	/\/\/\/\/\	10	10	100.00	0		
44	24/06/02	/\/\/\/\/\	10	10	100.00	0		
	Totals		348	348	100.00	0		

General principles of assessment :

a summary of key points

- There is a specific range of terminology associated with assessment.
- Assessment is an integral part of the teaching and learning process.
- Formative assessment is used to plan for effective teaching and learning.
- A variety of techniques can be used to collect information upon which to base judgements about progress and attainment, and by using a range of techniques you will gain a much better picture of a child's learning.
- Effective assessment must include children's self-assessment and evaluation.
- Marking children's work requires careful planning and must include feedback to the children.
- Record-keeping is a summary of assessment information that you will have as the teacher.
- Reporting to parents/carers needs to be informative and accurate, and to set targets for future learning.

Reflection point 2

At this point it is a good time to stop reading, reflect on your work so far and begin to plan the assessment that you will carry out in the next school placement.

Have your views of assessment changed now that you have been involved from the assessor end of the process? How does your assessment of learners compare with the assessment of yourself as a learner?

Statement	Yes	Not yet	Target	Notes
1. I have a copy of the assessment policy from my placement school or I have notes from reading this document.				
2. I have a copy of the marking policy or I have notes from reading this document.				
3. I know what the key objectives are that I will be teaching on the next placement.				
4. I have a plan of the assessment strategies I will try during this placement.				
5. I have some formats for record-keeping that I want to evaluate during this placement.				
6. I have discussed assessment with school-based staff.				
7. I have discussed whether or not there will be opportunities on this placement for being involved in statutory testing.				
8. I have seen the records of the children I will be teaching.				

You may not be preparing for a school placement but you may find it valuable to return to this reflection point just before your next visit to a school as part of your personal target-setting process. If your are in between placements it would be helpful to review your understanding of assessment terminology and perhaps visit some of the websites suggested at the back of this book to familiarise yourself with available resources.

2 ASSESSMENT IN PRIMARY ENGLISH

 2.1, 2.1b, 3.2.1, 3.2.2, 3.2.3, 3.2.4, 3.2.6

Trainees must demonstrate:

- *secure knowledge and understanding of the English National Curriculum and the framework, methods and expectations set out in the National Literacy Strategy;*
- *the use of a range of monitoring and assessment strategies to evaluate children's progress towards planned learning objectives, and the use of this information to improve their own planning and teaching and to give immediate feedback;*
- *their ability to evaluate and assess their teaching and their children's learning in English, including marking and giving appropriate feedback;*
- *their ability to assess speaking and listening, reading, spelling and writing;*
- *their ability to assess children's progress in English using the relevant National Curriculum level descriptors;*
- *their ability to identify and support more able children, and those working below age-related expectations;*
- *their ability to record children's progress and achievement in English systematically to provide evidence of the range of work, progress and attainment over time and to use this to help children review their own progress and to inform planning.*

You may find it helpful to read through the appropriate section of the Handbook that accompanies the Standards for the award of QTS for further clarification and support.

Introduction

Assessment is an integral part of effective teaching in English, as in every other area of the curriculum, but assessing English is more complicated than assessing other subjects. Assessing children's attainments and monitoring their progress in English involves teachers and children in a variety of oral and written processes, designed to assist in judgements about children's performance in speaking, listening, reading and writing, in a range of styles and genres for a range of audiences and purposes.

This chapter sets out to assist you in making assessments in all aspects of children's learning in English. It will seek to address the issues you will face in relation to:

- **speaking and listening;**
- **reading with accuracy and fluency;**
- **reading with understanding;**
- **spelling;**
- **handwriting;**
- **target-setting for writing;**
- **writing in different genres;**
- **grammar for writing;**

- children's involvement in assessing writing;
- marking and feedback.

Speaking and listening

With only passing reference to speaking and listening in the NLS, you will need to refer to the National Curriculum guidance in English, which describes what children should be taught in the areas of speaking, listening, group discussion and interaction, drama, standard English and language variation at both key stages. These descriptions convert readily into statements of how children behave as speakers and listeners, as in this example of a record of children's observed behaviour at Key Stage I.

Speaking and Listening – Record of assessments – Key Stage 1		
Name:	Year:	
Knowledge, skills and understanding	*Date and type of activity observed*	*Comments of observer*
Speaking • Speaking clearly, with appropriate intonation. • Choosing precise words. • Being well organised. • Using only relevant detail. • Considering the needs of the audience.		
Listening • Keeping concentration. • Remembering points of interest. • Responding appropriately. • Using questions to aid understanding. • Listening to others' reactions.		
Group discussion and interaction • Listening to others and taking turns. • Giving reasons for views. • Taking different views into account.		
Drama • Creating and remaining in role. • Conveying characters and emotions. • Commenting constructively on drama.		
Standard English • Using some of the features of standard English.		
Language variation • Using different speech in different circumstances. • Adapting speech for the audience.		

In Key Stage I there are many opportunities to observe children speaking and listening in whole class, group and individual situations, but it does take some planning and organisation to ensure that you are able to devote yourself to the task in hand. You must be able to do this because observation is the only viable method of collecting evidence in this area.

Practical task

Try to decide what kinds of activities you would need to observe Key Stage 1 children engaged in, to provide evidence to support judgements about the knowledge, skills and understanding described in the first column of the Speaking and Listening Record of Assessments. The section in the National Curriculum guidance entitled 'Breadth of Study' may provide a useful starting point.

As this task was concerned with Key Stage I children, you might have considered such activities as circle-time talk, news, role play, puppets, story bags, reading aloud, ad hoc performances of songs, nursery rhymes and poems, show and tell, class assemblies, 'plan, do and review', visits and visitors, and guided reading and writing.

At Key Stage 2 it may seem more difficult to set up activities for the purpose of assessing speaking and listening but older children are usually just as willing to join in discussions in personal, social and health education (PSHE), tell everyone their latest news, read aloud, tell jokes and stories, perform in class assemblies, question visitors, interview friends and family, explain how they achieved something in science or worked out something in maths, or to contribute to guided reading and writing sessions.

There are, of course, some children who shy away from public contributions of any kind, whatever their key stage. For these children, individual and very small group activities must be planned. Other children may have specific difficulties, for example with presenting a persuasive argument, which will lead you to look in more detail at the evidence you have observed in order to diagnose exactly where the difficulties lie and how they might become a focus for your future teaching.

Yet others may have more general problems due to the fact that English is not their first language. You will need to talk to the Special Education Needs Coordinator (SENCO) or teacher with responsibility for English as an Additional Language (EAL) for help and support. Remember also that bilingualism can be something to be celebrated. Bilingual children will be just as articulate and confident in their home language as any other group, and all children, as well as teachers, can benefit from understanding this.

Having found evidence of the children's performance in particular observable activities and recorded it on some kind of proforma, similar to the example here, you can then turn to the level descriptions set out at the back of the National Curriculum guidelines. Attainment Target 1: Speaking and Listening describes the kinds of behaviour children will be exhibiting when they are working at certain levels. You then need to decide which level description best fits each child.

Attainment Target I: Speaking and Listening

LEVEL I

Pupils talk about matters of immediate interest. They listen to others and usually respond appropriately. They convey simple meanings to a range of listeners, speaking audibly, and begin to extend their ideas or accounts by providing some detail.

LEVEL 2

Pupils begin to show confidence in speaking and listening, particularly where the topics interest them. On occasions, they show awareness of the needs of the listener by including relevant detail. In developing and explaining their ideas they speak clearly and use a growing vocabulary. They usually listen carefully and respond with increasing appropriateness to what others say. They are beginning to be aware that in some situations a more formal vocabulary and tone of voice are used.

LEVEL 3

Pupils talk and listen confidently in different contexts, exploring and communicating ideas. In discussion, they show understanding of the main points. Through relevant comments and questions, they show they have listened carefully. They begin to adapt what they say to the needs of the listener, varying the use of vocabulary and the level of detail. They are beginning to be aware of standard English and when it is used.

If you have been working with Key Stage I children, it is likely that you will have to choose between these three level descriptions. The descriptions vary in terms of the children's confidence, their ability to move away from their own interests and towards the interests and needs of the listener, increasing appropriateness of response, quality and amount of vocabulary and an increasing realisation that formal situations require formal language. Not all of these elements may be observable in any one context, so it is important to understand that in making assessments about children's performance in speaking and listening, you are required to make 'best fit', not perfect judgements.

DRAMA

The National Curriculum and the National Literacy Strategy (NLS) require schools to teach children about making, presenting and responding to drama in both Key Stages I and 2. Drama is a practical activity, which can provide an exciting context for learning about plays and playscripts and for developing other literacy and personal and social skills. It can also prove to be an effective tool in the process of assessing not only speaking and listening but also reading comprehension and writing. How well a group of children performing a scene, which they have read, can help their peers to understand what the playwright is trying to put across is a clear indicator of how well they have understood the text themselves.

RESEARCH SUMMARY

Kempe (1999) has reported on a piece of small-scale research at Reading University, where groups of Years 5 and 6 children had been working on texts such as The Tempest and Hamlet to see if a practical approach would help the children to understand the narrative and the author's use of language.

Kempe found that as the children played with the words in the script, so they began to understand them more and their performances were capable of assisting their fellow pupils' understanding greatly.

Reading

The NLS tells us that children become successful readers by learning to use a range of strategies to get at the meaning of a text. It talks of these strategies being like searchlights shedding light upon the text. The searchlights are:

- **grammatical knowledge;**
- **word recognition and graphic knowledge;**
- **knowledge of context;**
- **phonic knowledge (sounds and spelling).**

The National Curriculum guidelines for English also suggest that these are the four elements of a reading strategy which children should be taught in order that they read with fluency, accuracy, understanding and enjoyment. It follows that if you are going to assess children's success in reading, you need to consider each of these elements.

Assessing accuracy and fluency in reading

Measuring children's accuracy and fluency is possible through the use of analysis of reading errors (miscue analysis or running record).

Miscue analysis works on the principle, as shown in Medwell, Wray, Minns, Griffiths and Coates (2002), that there is a reason for each of the mistakes a child makes when reading and an analysis of the reasons will give you a rational plan to work on for future success. For example, a child who is dependent on knowledge of context will make errors based on the words fitting into the meaning of the text, whether or not the words in the text look anything like the answers given, whereas a child who is dependent on phonic knowledge will give answers that sound similar to the missing words but which possibly make no sense in context. In each case a miscue analysis will tell you clearly where to direct your work with the child in future. A running reading record is an important part of the statutory assessment of reading at Key Stage I.

Practical task

Look at the statutory assessments in reading for Key Stage 1. You will see that there are written tests of reading comprehension and a reading task, which involves children in:

- *giving reasons for choosing a particular book;*
- *listening to the beginning of the book being read by the teacher;*

- *recalling events from that section;*
- *reading a selected passage which is marked on a running record;*
- *predicting what might happen next;*
- *describing personal reactions to the text.*

Read the guidance for teachers carefully. Look at the codes that are used in the running reading record. Think about the kinds of errors that children could make and what code you would record for each. Think about how the running record fits into the whole reading task.

Try this kind of reading task with a few children, either using the statutory materials or your own, but keep to the same methodology and coding system. Now consider how you could use the information you have found out about the children to aid their progress.

Assessing reading comprehension

Measuring children's understanding of what they have read is both more difficult and more interesting than assessing their fluency and accuracy. If you look at the reading comprehension National Test papers, both statutory and optional, used in Key Stage 2, you will see clearly that the written answers required of the children demand literacy skills well beyond those of accurate and fluent reading.

In its 'Implications for Teaching and Learning 2001', QCA reminds teachers that children achieving Level 4 in reading need to:

- **cross-relate information and ideas from different parts of the text;**
- **recognise and understand how different texts are structured;**
- **understand how layout and design features relate to specific purposes and effects;**
- **recognise when words or phrases have meanings beyond the literal and identify metaphorical or figurative meanings;**
- **infer and explain opinions and motives from dialogue, action and narration.**

Practical task

Look at the mark schemes for optional reading comprehension National Tests used in Key Stage 2. Go through each of the answers and, in each case, write down the focus of the question. You will quickly begin to see the literacy skills the children need to display in order to attempt the tests.

For example, in the Year 5 optional National Test 'Day of the Turtle' the focus of the questions includes:

- **inference;**
- **inference supported by textual evidence;**

- retrieval of detail;
- author's choice of language;
- interpretation;
- inference of character;
- understanding of themes;
- understanding of features of text type;
- understanding of presentational features;
- interpretation of textual detail;
- interpretation of information;
- deduction;
- inference of authorial viewpoint supported by textual evidence;
- personal response to viewpoints presented in the text.

Assessing reading comprehension in guided reading

During guided reading, teaching and assessment are inextricably linked. Guided reading sessions provide opportunities for the teacher and small groups of children to discuss together their understanding of a particular text. Questions posed by the teacher will not only support the children and aid their learning but will also provide valuable information about specific areas of difficulty, which need to be addressed for some or all of the children.

The success of this kind of teacher assessment is, of course, dependent on the quality and appropriateness of the questions. If you are going to use guided reading as an opportunity for assessing reading comprehension, then you must find an appropriately engaging and challenging text. Then you must carefully work out, in advance, the kinds of questions that will require the children to use skills such as inference, deduction and interpretation, which will demonstrate that they really do understand the text you have chosen.

The questions you prepare will need to be open-ended and designed to elicit answers relating to each of the literacy skills you are targeting in any particular text. They might include questions like the following:

- What does this tell us about the setting/character/event?
- Which words in the text make you think that?
- Why did this happen?
- What is the effect of these words?
- Why does the character do this? How do you know?
- Of which text type is this an example? Which features of the text type are shown here?
- How did the character feel when an event happened? What evidence can you find in the text to support your view?
- What were the relationships between the characters?
- What do you think would happen if ... ?
- Do you think it might have been different if ... ?
- Why did the author use that word or phrase? Why was it effective?
- Can you find a word in the text which means the same as ... ?
- What is the effect of this kind of layout?

Recording assessments from guided reading

The main purpose of this kind of teacher assessment in guided reading is to provide you with evidence that can inform your future planning for individuals, groups or whole classes. Having carefully decided on the skills you are targeting and the questions you will ask, any recording system you use therefore has simply to provide space for you to make brief comments about the particular successes or difficulties being experienced by individuals in the guided reading group, as shown in the example below.

Group Reading Record of assessments	Text: The Iron Man Date: 18th November Year: 5
Names of Children	**Comments of Observer**
Christopher	Fluent + accurate. Understanding of 'poetic' language. Interesting predictions.
Shannon	Halting - using a range of strategies to work out unfamiliar words.
Ravinder	Fluent. Good understanding of how the boy felt - could find evidence of feelings.
Daniel S.	Absent.
Sarah	Becoming more confident + fluent. Explained well why the Iron Man reacted as he did.
Jaspreet	Very fluent. Made interesting comments about difference between this part of text + video version.

Assessing reading comprehension through written questions

Just as in guided reading sessions, the quality of any written assessments you do is dependent upon the quality of the questions and the appropriateness of the chosen text. You need to choose fiction texts that make children interested in the unravelling of the plot and the relationships between the characters, or non-narrative texts that provide interesting information. Again, you need to be sure that the text will provide opportunities for you to ask questions and probe the range of the children's literacy skills, and that your questions are precisely worded so that there is no ambiguity about the skill each question is testing.

Practical task

Choose a text you think is appropriate for one of your literacy groups and write some questions to go with it. Make sure you include questions that require the children to use skills such as deduction, inference, understanding of themes, locating evidence, understanding the author's choice of language, understanding of text type and personal response as well as retrieval of detail.

Try out your reading comprehension test on a literacy group and design an assessment record for the children's results. Below is an example of such a record. It can be adapted to include those skills you have targeted in your test.

| Reading comprehension | | | | Text: | | | |
| Record of assessments | | | | Date: | | Year: | |

Names of children	Inference and deduction	Locating evidence	Author's choice of language	Retrieval of detail	Understanding of themes	Text type	Personal response

Comments:

Action:

Here is a completed record. Comments have been made only where they are really noteworthy and action will be taken as a result of the guided reading session.

Reading comprehension Record of assessments								Text: The Eighteenth Emergency (Betsy Byars) Date: 18th October Year: 5
Names of children	Inference and deduction	Locating evidence	Author's choice of language	Retrieval of detail	Understanding of themes	Text type	Personal response	
Christopher	✓✓✓	✓✓✓	✓✓	✓✓	✓✓✓✓	✓	✓✓✓	
Shannon	✓＊	✓✓✓	✓✓	✓✓	✓✓	✓	✓＊	
Ravinder	✓✓✓	✓✓✓	✓✓	✓✓	✓✓✓	✓	✓＊	
Daniel S.	＊	✓✓	✓✓	✓✓	✓✓	✓	✓＊	
Sarah	✓✓✓	✓✓✓	✓✓	✓✓·	✓✓✓✓	✓	✓✓✓	
Jaspreet	✓✓✓	✓✓✓	✓✓	✓✓	✓✓✓✓	✓	✓✓✓	

Comments

Shannon – Lack of understanding of the relationship between Mom and the boy & no appreciation of the cinematic quality of opening paragraph.

Ravinder – Ditto the opening.

Daniel S. – Ditto the opening. Found it v. difficult to imagine what might have happened to make the boy run or to understand what the relationship really was.

Action

① Talk generally about relationship between Mom and boy. Establish evidence for this and how to find it.

② Remember personal response problems when we compare Iron Man text and film. (Could look at Year 6 Sat. 'Leaving Home' for cinema comparison).

Spelling

Assessing spelling

Many strategies will play a part in the development of children's ability to spell accurately, but their relative importance will vary according to the age of the children. For example, understanding the division of words or syllables into onset (the beginning) and rime (the rest) will help young children attempt to spell new words which fit into a certain spelling pattern, whilst researching into the meanings of words beginning with 'ante' and suggesting opposites which begin with 'post' will be of interest and use to those in upper Key Stage 2. According to the NLS 'Phonics' document, as children move through Key Stages 1 and 2 the relative importance of the teaching strategies will shift from teaching phonics to the teaching of spelling conventions and rules, which will build on existing phonic knowledge. Assessment of spelling therefore needs to be appropriate to the teaching strategy being employed at any particular stage.

The NLS is quite explicit about what should be taught to children in each term of each year in relation to phonological awareness, phonics and spelling and word recognition, graphic knowledge and spelling for Key Stage 1 children, and spelling strategies, conventions and rules for Key Stage 2 children. This can prove very helpful as an agenda for assessment and recording.

Assessing phonics

It is essential to be aware of what children are being expected to learn through phonics before you can make any judgements about their success. According to the NLS, learning phonics should enable them to:

- **identify sounds in spoken words (phonological awareness);**
- **recognise the common spellings for each phoneme (phoneme–grapheme correspondence);**
- **blend phonemes into words for reading;**
- **segment words into phonemes for spelling.**

Progression in phonic skills and knowledge

The NLS suggests a seven-step progression in phonic skills and knowledge which the children should be taught. It provides a helpful, if rather rigid, framework for making assessments of the children's development. The activities it offers as teaching aids can be equally successful when used as devices for assessment.

For example, Step 2 requires the children to be able to pronounce phonemes correctly. One of the games you might use to teach this can also be used as a check on whether individual children can pronounce the phonemes accurately. The game is called Mood Sounds. The teacher says a phoneme and asks the children to repeat the sound as if they were angry, sad, happy, frightened, and so on. Groups or individuals can be asked to do this in order to ensure that all children can do it correctly. Small whiteboards can be used for various 'Show Me' games, which will enable you to see how well each child is developing in phoneme–grapheme correspondence. Letter fans, word cards, objects and hoops, sock puppets and washing lines can all be used to help you assess phonic skills and knowledge in an enjoyable way. For example, the children can use the letter fans to show you that they can spell particular phonemes, can distinguish the sound of one phoneme from another, can find the letter needed to finish the spelling of a word or can find the missing letter inside a word. Word cards can be used as 'flash' cards or for matching and sorting games. Hoops can be labelled so that children can put into them objects that contain certain phonemes in their names, or begin or end with certain letters. Sock puppets can be particularly helpful because they are allowed to be very silly creatures or alien beings who cannot pronounce things properly and have to be corrected by the children ... usually with great glee. A sock puppet can also provide the confidence needed to read or spell in front of the class. Washing lines, pegs and cards can be used for spelling CVCs, grouping words containing the same phoneme, alphabetical order, missing letters and many other activities which would normally be done with pencil and paper. The practical nature of 'pegging up the washing' makes it more enjoyable for the children and easier for you to see exactly who can do what.

The NLS expects children to learn how to blend words into phonemes for reading and how to segment words into phonemes for spelling.

RESEARCH SUMMARY

Goswami (1992) has shown clearly that young children find it very difficult to split a spoken word into separate phonemes and even more difficult to blend phonemes into whole words, but find it far less troublesome to split words or syllables into the onset and the rime. Goswami has further shown that where children have been taught to segment into onset and rime, they can use the knowledge they have to read new words with onsets and rimes they have met separately in other words.

Awareness and use of onset and rime is a stage which most children need to go through before they are able to segment words into phonemes, so you need to be careful when setting out to assess their development in this area of phonics. You may find that teaching and testing spellings within appropriate rimes is more successful for many young children than just lists of words containing the same sound.
For example:

Instead of – keen, sheet, weed, steel.
Try – keep, sheep, weep, steep.

Testing the spellings can be done by traditional spelling tests, or more enjoyably by completing rhyming couplets (e.g. Little Bo Peep, She had some ...), by changing the words in well-known rhymes or songs and asking the children to find the correct word, by finding the 'odd one out' in a list, or through other games and puzzles involving rhyming words. Of course, the best tests are for the children to write their own rhymes, or put their own rhyming word into incomplete texts, or simply to make use of the new spellings they have learned in their own unaided writing. This is not to say that spelling tests should not be employed at all but if you are going to use them, be clear about what they are for. If spellings are sent home to be learned as homework, spelling tests can support that and help you to keep an eye on individual children's participation and progress, but they are not central to the teaching and learning of spellings.

Key Stage 2 children in many schools have a spelling journal (see NLS Spelling Bank Appendix 6) in which they write up investigations into derivations, roots and meanings of words as well as lists of words with common prefixes, suffixes or spelling patterns and words arranged according to the device by which the children can remember them, such as mnemonics or specific spelling rules. You can assess the competence of such children by testing or by setting investigations, word games, crossword puzzles, dictionary work, making a thesaurus, and so on, or by setting the children individual targets for their unaided writing. You should encourage the children to assess their own spelling, both at the redrafting and final stages of their writing, having made explicit the level of accuracy you require of them.

Practical task

Look at the NLS 'Spelling Bank: List of words and activities for the Key Stage 2 spelling objectives'. Read Year 3 Term 1: Objective 11 on page 7. Think about how you could use some of the suggested activities to assess children's spelling of words with prefixes 'un' and 'dis'.

Handwriting

The NLS makes clear that children should begin to write in a joined style from Year 2 and that their progress towards fluency and legibility in that style should be complete by the end of Year 4. In reality there are some children who are not ready to begin the process in Year 2 and others who have been taught joined handwriting from their introduction to writing in Reception. In Key Stage 2 there are many children who still need to practise their handwriting beyond Year 4.

Children need to be able to produce different types of writing for different purposes. These include:

- **a fluent, joined, legible script for everyday use;**
- **a way of writing quickly which is clear to the writer, for making notes;**
- **'best handwriting' which shows off the writer's style;**
- **appropriate scripts for labels, captions, headings, posters, etc.**

Any assessments you make about the children's handwriting must take into account their age and stage of development, which will depend on their previous experience and the purpose for which they are writing.

It is very easy to be subjective when assessing handwriting. You may prefer a style that is similar to your own, or object to a style where the letters seem to fall backwards, but you must remember that you should be looking for consistency in:

- **letter formation;**
- **spacing;**
- **orientation;**
- **size;**
- **joins.**

Practical task

Collect some examples of 'best handwriting'. Ask the teachers in your school if you can look at examples of handwriting from three children in each of their classes (a good, middle and not so good). Look at the development of the good writers from Reception to Year 6, the 'middle' writers and the 'not so good'. How do they compare in terms of letter formation, spacing, orientation, size and, where appropriate, joins? Use the National Curriculum for English level descriptions as a general guide and assign a level to each piece of work.

Writing

Anecdotal evidence from teachers shows that assessing children's writing is among the most difficult assessment tasks they have to undertake. When all the staff or groups of teachers get together to moderate children's writing, it is rare that they come to agreement about the levels children are working at without considerable and lengthy discussion. Disagreements generally result from people allowing subjective judgements to intervene when they should be judging against objective criteria, or being unsure about what relative weight to give to the content, organisation, language and presentational aspects of the writing.

As a teacher, you will have to assess each and every element in children's writing, so it is vital that both you and the children are quite clear about the particular elements you are assessing at any given time. However it is also important that you begin by accepting that you will have an instinctive reaction to any piece of writing, which will lead you to a general view about the kind of level at which the child is working. This can be a useful starting point for more detailed assessments and for target-setting.

Using target-setting in assessing writing

Target-setting is an integral and vital part of the assessment process which will inform future work with individuals, groups and whole classes of children and which provides opportunities for children to take some responsibility for their own learning. Before you can plan effectively for children's future writing development, you have to know 'where the children are'. This necessarily involves some kind of assessment, which can be done quickly and easily from children's unaided writing.

Practical task

Read the level descriptions that relate to writing (Attainment target 3) in the National Curriculum. These are very general statements and they are helpful for making initial judgements about children's writing. They should help you to get a 'feel' for the levels at which children are working and they can be easily adapted to produce a checklist against which general or initial assessments can be made.

Writing	Name:	Date:
Record of assessments		Year:

General level	Fiction	Non-fiction
Level 1	Simple words and phrases for meaning Starting to be aware of full stops Letters usually clearly shaped and correctly orientated	Simple words and phrases for meaning Starting to be aware of full stops Letters usually clearly shaped and correctly orientated
Level 2	Appropriate and interesting vocabulary for meaning Ideas in sequence Some sentences with full stops and capital letters Simple words correctly spelt Handwriting accurate	Appropriate and interesting vocabulary for meaning Ideas in sequence Some sentences with full stops and capital letters Simple words correctly spelt Handwriting accurate
Level 3	Organised and imaginative Interesting words Some understanding of sentence structure Spelling usually accurate Punctuation of sentences Handwriting joined and legible	Basic features of different genres Sequences of sentences logical Some understanding of sentence structure Spelling usually accurate Punctuation of sentences Handwriting joined and legible
Level 4	Lively and thoughtful Organised for the reader Precise, imaginative vocabulary Use of complex sentences Range of punctuation Handwriting in own fluent style	Formal language where appropriate Layout and conventions relate to text type Use of complex sentences Range of punctuation Handwriting in own fluent style
Level 5	Sophisticated in form and style Extended engagement of the reader Use of paragraphs Complex words spelt correctly Range of less common punctuation Handwriting adapted to task	Layout and conventions entirely appropriate to text type Sentence construction to suit genre Precise or technical language Complex words spelt correctly Handwriting adapted to task Understanding of the needs of the reader

The kind of checklist shown here can help you to begin the 'assessment, planning, review' cycle, which is essential for effective teaching and learning. When you have assigned general, 'gut reaction' levels to examples of the children's unaided writing, you will have a fair idea of 'where the children are' and can compare that with 'where they should be', as shown in the more detailed National Literacy Strategy document *Target statements for writing* (2000). You then need to look for common trends, which show up across a whole class. These will help you in your future planning for whole class teaching and will determine the targets you set your class – targets which need to be explicit, visible, taught and assessed and which might involve children making judgements about their own success.

Further analysis of the general levels ascribed to the children's unaided writing should lead you to grouping children by ability and the setting of group targets, which will become the focus of your work in guided writing and which may lead on to individual targets for children during particular writing activities.

Records of children's achievements during guided writing should also include future group targets and any notes you feel it appropriate to make about individual children's needs. You can then talk privately to those children and with them devise individual targets for their future writing. Figure 2.1 is a narrative writing record to use with children who are writing at level 4 and working towards level 5. It includes all aspects of writing: purpose and organisation, style, punctuation, spelling and handwriting.

Narrative Writing Record   (Adapted from writing record produced by Coventry Education Support and Advisory Service)

Narrative Writing Level 4 towards Level 5 Term/date Names	Children in a group can	Purpose and organisation				Style			Punctuation			Spelling			Handwriting	
		Write in a definite genre e.g.fable.	Write in appropriate paragraphs.	Mix action, description and dialogue.	Include thoughts and feelings for character.	Use variety of simple and complex sentences.	Choose imaginative vocabulary for a particular effect.	Use similes and metaphors.	Use commas, inverted commas etc.	Use apostrophes for omission & possession.	Use brackets and dashes.	Apply independent spelling strategies.	Build words from other known words – from meaning or derivation.	Apply known prefixes, suffixes and letter strings for new words.	Use fluent, joined handwriting.	Display own style consistently.
Future targets for the group					Notes on individual children											

Figure 2.1: Narrative writing record.

This process may be summarised as follows:

Look at children's unaided writing.

Assign a 'gut feeling' level to each piece.

Talk positively about what has already been achieved.

Identify trends that are common across the whole class and decide on class targets to be addressed in whole class teaching.

Group children by ability and set targets, which will be central to group teaching in guided writing sessions.

Record the children's achievements during guided writing and decide on future group targets.

Make notes on individual children and discuss future objectives with them.

For the children to become successful writers, it is essential that they feel part of this whole process and do not simply become involved at the point where they receive targets set by someone else, for no apparent reason. Their involvement must begin with understanding the purpose of their original unaided writing and they must share in the celebration of what they have already achieved. Then they need to see how you have reached your decisions about class and group targets and the role you are going to play in helping them achieve these goals. At this point you can display class and group targets in the classroom and provide individual children with targets written in their exercise books or on small cards such as bookmarks.

RESEARCH SUMMARY

Clarke has written extensively about the importance of sharing the learning intention, success criteria and ASIDE with the children.

- *Learning intention: target, what is hoped will be learned.*
- *Success criteria: the measures of success, how we can judge success.*
- *ASIDE: the context or general reason for doing the work.*

This is an example of learning intention, success criteria and ASIDE used with Key Stage I children from 'Unlocking Formative Assessment' (2001).

> **Learning intention in the teacher's plan: to explore narrative order and identify and map out the main stages of a story.**
>
> **Shared with the children:**
> Learning intention: We are learning to order our own and other stories.
> Success criteria: We will have ordered the story we looked at into our own story plan.
> ASIDE (oral only): Ordering is an important skill in reading, writing and maths.

Following her work with the Gillingham Partnership schools, Clarke reported that teachers felt that children's awareness of the learning intention, success criteria and ASIDE:

- *helped them to try to meet the success criteria;*
- *guided their thoughts before they started;*
- *sharpened their focus;*
- *made them more able to talk about their work and ask for clarification;*
- *assured that having the learning intention and success criteria visible meant that they referred to them during the lesson.*

(Clarke, S., Lopez-Charles, G. and McCallum, G. 2001, p. 30)

Children's involvement in assessing writing

Specific target-setting not only makes assessment easier for the teacher by providing objective criteria against which to make judgements, but it also makes it possible for children to ask themselves whether they think they have been successful in what they set out to achieve.

RESEARCH SUMMARY

Clarke's work in Gillingham (Clarke et al., 2001) also shows that where children have been shown the appropriate questions to consider through modelling, they can be successfully involved in self- and peer evaluation. Typical questions were:

- *What did you find easy/hard about … ?*
- *How would you do things differently next time?*
- *What can you do now that you couldn't do before?*
- *What do you need to move on to now?*
- *What do you need more help with about learning to … ?*

The extent of children's involvement and the manner of their recording will depend on their age and experience but most children should be able to be involved at some level. Figure 2.2 is an example of a record to be kept by a child working at Level 3b. As each statement is achieved, a tongue of flame is appropriately coloured.

Figure 2.2: a record of story skills at level 3b.

Another way for the children to keep a record of their own achievements is to turn their targets into 'I can' statements and then write, draw or stick them on to their record book, sheet or poster. Here are two examples, one for Year 1 and one for Year 6:

> I am learning to write in short sentences or groups of words.

> I can write in short sentences or groups of words.

> My target is to show significant interaction between characters, saying how they feel and react.

> In my writing, I have demonstrated significant interaction between characters, saying how they feel and react.

Assessing different elements in children's writing

ASSESSING DIFFERENT GENRES
The targets you set for children in their writing are the targets against which you will be making judgements, so the children must understand exactly what is required of them in terms of the genre in which they are to write. This presupposes a sufficiently wide experience of studying a range of texts and seeing writing modelled in a range of different genres.

RESEARCH SUMMARY

Christie (1995) suggests from her research into the writing development of 55 children from entry into Reception until the end of Year 2 that children are being 'confined' to the genre of recount and that teachers believe personal experience provides children with sufficient content about which to talk and write. She argues that recounts – involving the simplest reconstruction of personal experience – are arguably the most commonly produced written genres in primary school education. In the particular study she undertook, the children wrote a very large number of texts using the same basic generic structure throughout Years 1 and 2 of schooling.

By the end of Key Stage 2, children should be familiar with a range of fiction and non-fiction genres, which might include:

Fiction
Diary, fairy tale, humour, adventure, science fiction, fantasy, ghost, mystery, romance, myth, legend, fable, comedy and tragedy.

Non-fiction
Information, report, recount, instruction, persuasion, discussion, directory, journal, biography, letter and diary.

Practical task

Identify the genre of each:

- *a poster advertising a theme park;*
- *a description of a football match in a newspaper;*
- **The Hare and the Tortoise;**
- *an entry in an encyclopaedia about volcanoes;*
- *a recipe;*
- **Cider with Rosie.**

You may find it helpful to read Lewis and Wray, **Writing Frames** *(1996) before you try to identify the specific genres.*

If you are assessing children's writing in a particular genre, you will be looking for the elements of style and form which characterise that genre. For example, if the children have been writing a report, you will be checking that they have used:

- **present tense;**
- **a description of how things are;**
- **a general introduction;**
- **more detail as the report develops.**

If they have been writing a legend, you will be looking for:

- **a main character and companions from the past;**
- **the good, honest and brave fighting against evil and injustice;**
- **contact with magical artefacts or characters with supernatural powers;**
- **just the possibility that the story could be true;**
- **consistent use of past tense and third person.**

Apart from looking at their writing, another way to assess children's understanding of different genres is to ask them to draw concept maps. A concept map is a kind of flow diagram with a particular genre in the centre, surrounded by all the elements associated with it, relating to its organisation, style and punctuation. Concept maps can also be used to test the quality of teaching in respect of a certain writing genre. By asking the children to draw a concept map before you begin a section of work on that genre and again at the end of the work, you can judge how successful your teaching has been.

Practical task

When you next have to teach report-writing, myths or any other genre, start by asking the children to put what they already know onto a concept map. At the end of the work, repeat the concept maps and you should have a fairly clear idea of what you have taught and the children have learned.

Assessing grammar for writing

It appears that after each set of Key Stage I and Key Stage 2 National Test papers has been marked, QCA reports that writing 'lags behind' reading. In January 2002, QCA identified the two most significant issues as the use of full stops and capital letters and the quality of narrative writing. The use of full stops and capital letters was 'not sufficiently secure' and there was some evidence that accurate use had declined. QCA recommended that children should be taught more clearly the use of full stops in complex sentences and the use of paragraphing to link action, motive and setting. The DfEE has said that writing will continue to lag behind until children are made more aware of key grammatical principles and their effects, in order to increase the range of choices open to them when they write.

According to the DfEE publication *Grammar for Writing* (2000), the teaching of writing should start from:

* **exploration of written texts to identify some important grammatical choices writers have made to achieve their purpose, e.g. choice of verbs, use of pronouns, sentence structure;**
* **active investigation of these grammatical features to explore their effects;**
* **application of these features through teacher-led shared writing;**
* **use of shared writing as a framework for independent writing supported through group guided writing.**

This methodology will succeed where children are given opportunities to discuss language and have the means and technical understanding to do so, and where they are being made aware of the differences between spoken and written language patterns. They need to realise that their written language must be more explicit, orga-nised and coherent than their spoken language if their audience is to be clear about the meaning of their written texts.

The DfEE guidance also talks about setting clear grammar targets for children in order to explain what they are expected to learn about writing and to involve them in evalu-ating their own work. It cites 'we can ... ' statements as helpful in enabling children to gain control, aim for specific improvements in their own work and earn the credit for success. It gives the following examples:

* **We can use a capital letter and full stop to punctuate a sentence. (Year I)**
* **We can write complex sentences using a wide range of subordinates, such as because, although, while and since. (Year 5)**

No doubt grammar targets can be just as effective as the learning intentions discussed earlier, but beware too many targets. Children could drown beneath a welter of targets for style, organisation, vocabulary, grammar, spelling, handwriting, etc. if you are not careful.

Practical task

*Read Parts 1 and 2 of The National Literacy Strategy document entitled **Grammar for Writing (2000). Look at the teaching unit on page 48. It is designed to help children in Year 3 Term 1 to begin to organise stories into paragraphs. Understanding paragraphing in narrative writing is an extremely important step for a developing writer, so it is vital that we as teachers are clear about our children's present understanding. Think about how you could use this unit to help you assess the understanding of a class of Year 3 children and how you might involve the children in this assessment.***

Throughout the *Grammar for Writing* document, there are activities that can be used equally successfully for teaching and for assessing children's grammatical knowledge and understanding, and which lend themselves to the involvement of children in self-evaluation.

Making formal assessments of children's writing

Making a formal assessment of a child's writing and giving it an overall level to reflect the content and organisation, style, punctuation, spelling and handwriting will never-theless be, as it is for all teachers, a daunting task. If you have a placement in either Year 2 or Year 6 you may see preparations for, or the administration of, National Tests. If you are in any other year group in Key Stage 2, you may see optional National Tests being used. Most schools now make use of them to track children's progress, and some report the results to parents. Make sure you take any opportunity to be involved with this formal assessment of children's work.

In relation to writing, you will find the guidance for teachers in the National Test mate-rials very helpful. Make sure you look at the guidance for each year group and get used to analysing children's writing using the analysis sheets available in each book. Alternatively, you could devise your own to include all the elements you particularly wish to assess. Figure 2.4 is an example of an analysis sheet, which has been adapted from the National Tests materials. It is designed to help the teacher note any evidence of achievement in a piece of narrative writing. The list of cues can be altered to reflect the age of the child and the expectations of the teacher. This analysis sheet has been completed after reading Rhiannon's story, which is also reproduced here.

Thursday 9th January 03.

A change in time

She looked around. Nothing was the same.
"Where—" she was suddenly pulled back, her baggy jeans caught a stone and ripped.
"What are you doing!" began a terrified small, thin girl. She was about Sam's age and looked hot and sweaty.

Sam realised she was being pulled into a deep hole, she tripped and fell, but she caught a sight of men in green uniform over the other side of what looked like a village square.

"The Nanzi's are, there (are) you're just standing a few feet behing them, havent you a (brain) brain!" She said this fast and in a posh sort of voice.

Excuse "Icscuise-me", Sam said in a nervoust voice, "Umm, who are you?"

"Ow, sorry, my name is Sirillar. Have no Idear what the rest is. I'm an orphan, see."

"Oww, sorry." Sam said, in what she thought was a sympthetic voice.

"Ow, no worries. They died when I was a baby. I just ranaway from (them) my orphanige.
Sam gasped. "Wont they look for you—probably"

"Ow, of course not, they wont care, proberly wont even know I'm gone!" She said this in a cheery expression.

Sam picked up a newspaper, the date said 1940, she read out the heading, "WAR STRIKES TERROR ONCE AGAIN"
Sam suddenly realised what had happened, "I've gone back in time to the Second World War!" Sirillar raised her eyebrows

Figure 2.3: Rhiannon's story.

and picked up the book. She gave a gasp. "I wrote this book, before I ran-away, I left it by a fairground, by a gypsy jypsey woman, a fortune teller, It's just like whats happening now, but that means, ow know" she whispered to Sam, "the Nanzis are listening to everyword we're saying, we've got to run, or –

"they'll get the book, go to the future and take over the world –

"AAhhhh", Serillar let out a petrified, scream, 8 Nanzis had just leapt into the small den in which Sirillar used as a hideout when the blitz started. "Open the book" She screamed,

"No, it will take all of us, and I can't leave you, you'll die!"
"We have to get away, on our own and open the book," Serillar screamed through a bleeding nose.

"OK," Sam shouted, she kicked and pushed punched and bit, this was no time to be ladylike, she had to fight for her life! She grabbed Serillas hand, pushed the last remaining Nanzi, (with some difficulty) and, with Serillas help, pushed the Nanzi against the wall where long trickles of blood emerged from his hair.
They helped eachother out and opened the book. a loud whooshing noise told them they were going back, or were they?

Analysis Sheet: Narrative Writing

Child's Name: _Rhiannon_   Year _6_   Date _9.1.03_

Definite genre and theme

Rhiannon was obviously asked to write a 'time-slip' story and she has made it clear throughout.

Paragraphs

She is using paragraphs to organise her story but she does not indent for each new speaker in dialogue.

Description of setting and characters

Little description of setting but the characters develop well with small insights into their personalities + background as the story progresses.

Dialogue

Dialogue is realistic and helps to move the story forward – it also provides background information.

Other elements e.g. humour, detail, persuasiveness

Humour – "this was no time to be ladylike".
Use of newspaper to indicate new time + place.
Idea of Nazis using book to go to the future + take over the world.

Range of different kinds of sentences

Simple, compound and complex sentences... but some sentences wrongly punctuated – use of comma where capital + full stop should have been used.

Vocabulary/figurative language

No simile or metaphor. Some good vocabulary – nervous, sympathetic, posh voice; cheery expression; petrified scream; through a bleeding nose; long trickles of blood emerged from his hair.

Punctuation

Over use of comma – wrongly use to demarcate sentences. Generally correct use of speech marks.

Spelling

Most common polysyllabic words spelt correctly. Some errors relate to speech e.g. excuse, probably.

Handwriting

Appropriate for a first draft, time limited story.

Figure 2.4: A completed analysis sheet for Rhiannon's story.

Practical task

Read Rhiannon's story and the analysis sheet that accompanies it. Then read Kurt's story (below) and use the blank analysis sheet to make comments under each heading.

- Genre – Is the theme of the story clear?
- Paragraphs – Does he use paragraphs correctly for demarcation and for dialogue?
- Description – Are the setting and characters sufficiently described?
- Dialogue – Is the dialogue meaningful and its punctuation correct?
- Other elements – Is there any humour? Does it provoke any emotion?
- Sentences – Is there a mixture of simple, compound and complex sentences?
- Vocabulary/figurative language – Does he use interesting words? Are there similes, metaphors, personification?
- Punctuation – Is the punctuation correct? Does he use dashes, brackets, and ellipses?
- Spelling – Does he spell correctly polysyllabic words that follow patterns? Does he make use of knowledge of prefixes and suffixes?
- Handwriting – Is it joined, fluent, legible and appropriate to the task?

> Thursday 9th January 2003
> Prisoner - a change in time
> Sam was bored. For the last five minutes he had just been walking up and down the hall. His Playstation 2 wasn't working and none of his friends wanted to have a game of football.
> Suddenly Sam looked down. He had stumbled over a book. An extremely thick book. It would take a madman to sit down and write a book like that and just as madman to sit down and read it, Sam thought. It was titled 'Incredible History'. Sam liked history. He opened the book, And felt as if he had blacked out for a split second. Everything had gone black anyway.
> He had only just realised that the book was no longer in his hands. What had happened when he blacked out? He was still in the same position. And then his jaw dropped and his eyes bulged as he suddenly realised he was in a desert, like ancient

Figure 2.5: Kurt's story.

Egypt. But in a way it was so much different. It was like a cross between Ancient Egypt and Ancient Rome.

'There he is!' Yelled a voice. Sam span round to see three soldiers running towards him. He started to run. But the soldiers were too fast. All of a sudden, they were on top of him, and the last thing Sam saw was the handle of a blade crashing towards his face.

Sam awoke. He had a giant bruise to the left of his forehead and an open cut (which was very wide) running from his right eye to his left nostril. And he was in agony.

He was overwhelmed. By the pain, but also who he was. All of a sudden he was an adult who was a criminal who was on the run. Sam didn't understand. He was 12 years old, and had never stolen anything in his life. He was actually a very honest boy. It was like he had switched bodies, or was it real? It had to be

He was in a small cell. He had a bed in the corner which was muddy and torn. There was no way out. The door was locked. In front of the door (of the door) was a giant of a man with a large moustache. He was wearing a Roman soldier uniform, complete with helmets. In his hand he carried a short, blood-stained blade with a curve. Sam noticed it had been sharpened. He was terrified.

'Damn!' he meant to shout but the words came out in a speak. It felt like he had a pebble stuck in his throat.

'It's a bit late for that,' The soldier had a load, drony, sarcastic voice. 'I'm General Simone, general of King Thierry's army. And I'm not gonna stop guarding this cell.' Sam flung himself on the bed and heard the clang of (steel) x steel. It gave him an idea.

He rested his palms on the bottom of the bed. It was steel. Switching bodies with an adult had strengthened him. He span it at the door. His idea worked. These cells were quickly built. A bad idea. With a clatter the door fell down. General Simone screamed as it landed on top of him. Sam wrenched the sword out of his broken arm. He started to run. But one of the general's arm's were free. He hung on to Sam's leg and brought him down. Sam did what he had to do, and the scream coming from the general was what gave him away.

He sprinted as fast as he could, guards following his every step. Soon Sam was out of breath and came to a bridge, where he stopped. The guards closed in. With the rest of his strength he fought, but very soon his sword was flicked off the bridge. The bridge was about 200 metres high. He was beaten. He slumped against a rock. And very slowly, the guards closed in.

Analysis Sheet: Narrative Writing

Child's name: Year: Date:

Definite genre and theme:

Paragraphs:

Description of setting and characters:

Dialogue:

Other elements e.g. humour, detail, persuasiveness:

Range of different kinds of sentences:

Vocabulary/figurative language:

Punctuation:

Spelling:

Handwriting:

Marking and feedback

Having ensured that the children were quite clear about the expectations you had of them for their writing, whether the targets you set were class, group or individual targets, and whether they related to genre, grammar, spelling or handwriting or any mixture of these, you have to decide how you are going to feed back to each child the results of your assessment of their work.

All children are entitled to a comment about their efforts and it makes sense that such comments should relate directly to the targets they have been working towards. However, it is not physically possible to feed back at length and in any great detail to all children each time they write. You have therefore to make decisions about priorities. You may wish to concentrate on a group of children who are all working on the same targets. You may feel that the more or least able children are your priority at a particular time. What is important is that the children are aware of the group you are concentrating on and why.

Your focus group can then be given detailed comments on their writing and the extent to which you feel they have achieved their objectives. This can be done through written remarks, provided the children are old enough to be able to understand them. Any criticism should be constructive, include explanations of how to improve the work, and be linked to any future targets the children are to be given.

For the rest of the children, your marking can be much more cursory and may result in general comments given orally to the whole class.

RESEARCH SUMMARY

The LEARN Project – Guidance for Schools on Assessment for Learning, University of Bristol – CLIO Centre for Assessment Studies (June 2000) found that children saw feedback as a crucial element in helping them improve their work. Most primary school children only received positive comments and preferred oral to written remarks. Constructive criticism was helpful if it aided children's understanding of what the task required and wasn't interpreted as a personal attack. All children felt positive comments boosted their confidence but, although ticks, smiley faces and 'good work' signified approval, they didn't help children to 'bridge the gap' between present performance and future goals.

Assessment in primary English :

a summary of key points

- *Assessing English involves teachers and children in a range of oral and written processes.*
- *Observation is the only viable method of collecting evidence of children's progress in speaking and listening.*
- *Children's accuracy and fluency in reading can be judged by using a running reading record or miscue analysis.*
- *Successful assessment of reading comprehension is dependent on the quality and appropriateness of the oral or written questions teachers pose.*
- *Target-setting is an integral and vital part of the assessment of writing, in which children can have an important role.*

■ *Careful analysis of children's writing, against clearly defined criteria, should be undertaken before assigning any formal level of attainment.*

■ *Spelling tests can be a helpful guide but are not central to the teaching and learning of spelling.*

■ *Assessment of children's handwriting should be objective and take account of the purpose of the writing.*

■ *Quality feedback is a crucial element in improving children's writing.*

Reflection point 3

At this point it is a good time to stop reading and reflect upon your work so far, but this time with specific reference to a subject – English.

- *Have your views of assessment in English changed now that you have been involved from the assessor end of the process?*
- *How does your assessment of learners compare with the assessment of you as a learner in English?*
- *Have you established clear priorities for assessment strategy of English?*
- *Will you be focusing on all aspects of English during your next placement or do you have related course-based tasks in a specific area, e.g. reading?*
- *What subject knowledge might you need in order to identify potential difficulties that children could have with areas you are going to be teaching, e.g. spelling patterns or writing genres?*

Statement	Yes	Not yet	Target	Notes
1. I have a copy of the English subject policy from my placement school or I have notes from reading this document specifically focusing on the assessment section.				
2. I have a copy of the marking policy or I have notes from reading this document specifically related to the teaching and learning of English.				
3. I know what the key objectives for English are that I will be teaching on the next placement.				
4. I have a plan of the assessment strategies I will try during this placement.				
5. I have some formats for record-keeping for specific aspects of English that I want to evaluate during this placement.				
6. I have discussed assessment with school-based staff.				
7. I have discussed whether or not there will be opportunities on this placement for being involved in statutory testing in English.				
8. I have seen the records for English of the children I will be teaching.				

Introduction

This chapter will consider assessment issues specifically in mathematics. These will be the issues that arise in mathematics which don't emerge in other subjects in the same way. What makes assessing mathematics different from other subjects? Many people think of mathematics as having either 'right' or 'wrong' answers and therefore as being relatively easy to assess. With the introduction of the National Numeracy Strategy (NNS), however, the emphasis on mathematics teaching and learning has changed, and with it, the expectations of teachers' assessments. The mental/oral work requires different assessment strategies from marking written calculations. This chapter will look specifically at some of the assessment issues as they relate to mathematics, including using and applying mathematical knowledge. At the beginning of the chapter is a summary of the requirements of the Qualifying to Teach document published by the Teacher Training Agency (TTA). You should reflect on these as you read the chapter and think about how you can achieve these standards in relation to teaching numeracy.

A summary is then given of the assessment requirements stated in the National Numeracy Strategy Framework. The requirement of the National Curriculum will be considered in conjunction with addressing error and misconceptions. A variety of assessment tools will be examined and the latest developments in assessment will be addressed.

Practical task

With regard to mathematics lessons, how could you provide evidence that you are addressing the Standards summarised at the beginning of the chapter? You will need a copy of the Standards to assist you with this question.

Perhaps the easiest of these to provide evidence for is 3.3.2, 'Trainees can teach the required or expected knowledge, understanding and skills relevant to the curriculum for pupils in the age range for which they are trained', as this could be observed during a numeracy lesson. In order to teach effectively you must know what children's prior knowledge of mathematics is and any errors and misconceptions they may have, so that you can plan in a focused way to promote progress in learning. Addressing misconceptions, which are experienced by individuals, groups or the whole class, could provide evidence. The others could be assessed over a period of time, but initially help would be needed with training to achieve these.

Why do we assess mathematics?

We assess mathematics to ensure that there is progression and achievement. Teachers need to know whether children:

- **have attained mathematical knowledge;**
- **have acquired the necessary skills to complete a task;**
- **have developed concepts that will help them to understand mathematical ideas and processes;**
- **can build on known fact to acquire derived facts;**
- **can organise information in order to successfully complete a problem-solving exercise;**
- **can be flexible in their approaches to problem-solving;**
- **have a positive attitude to mathematics;**
- **understand mathematical language;**
- **can identify connections between different areas of mathematics;**
- **can identify and explain patterns in number;**
- **can predict an outcome from evidence already gathered;**
- **can make informed decisions.**

When considering at the most effective assessment in numeracy teachers must be assured that it promotes children's learning.

Assessment for learning is any assessment for which the priority in its design is to serve the purpose of promoting pupils' learning. It differs from assessment designed primarily to serve the purposes of accountability, or of ranking, or of certifying competence.

(Black, Harrison, Lee, Marshall and Wiliam, 2002)

Assessment within the National Curriculum is mentioned earlier in this book. However, the National Numeracy Framework for Teaching Mathematics Reception to Year 6 is quite specific (pages 33 to 37). In summary, the NNS Framework states that assessment, recording and reporting are important elements of teaching, but they must be manageable if the information is to be useful to you, to others and to the children. It suggests that assessment should be regarded as planning in that there should be short-term assessment, medium-term assessment and long-term assessment. Assessment should inform your teaching plans at all levels and become part of the cycle of planning, teaching and assessment.

Short-term assessment

Short-term planning should be an integral part of each numeracy lesson. The purpose is to:

- **check that children have understood the main teaching points;**
- **check that children are remembering number facts and can use mental strategies;**
- **use the information you have gained to help you to adjust day-to-day plans and brief any support staff or other adult helpers who are working with the children.**

You need to assess if the learning objectives are being achieved during the lesson by absorbing and reacting to children's responses. You also need to assess whether those who are hesitant with new work require more teaching input, or those who are confident need more extension work. With four groups operating in the class you may decide to target a different group daily and by informal questioning check that skills, knowledge and understanding are being acquired. At intervals you can also check informally, by setting an out-of-class homework or an informal test. You should respond to these sort of assessments immediately by marking and discussion with the whole class in order to give children feedback on their performance and guidance about what they need to do to improve. At the same time any errors and misconceptions can be addressed in a non-threatening way, and it is also a useful way to bring the whole class together.

Observing children and listening to them during the numeracy hour can aid with formative or short-term assessment. Watching Reception children count can reveal many misconceptions and errors – for example, they may just be reciting the numbers and not yet have achieved one-to-one correspondence, they may repeat numbers, or miss numbers out, or not be secure in the sequencing. Lisa, a Reception child, was asked by a trainee teacher how she was counting the objects and Lisa replied 'on my legs'. A somewhat bemused trainee though that she probably meant using her toes. She questioned the child further, but to the trainee's surprise Lisa explained that for every object she counted she bounced her legs.

Formative assessment includes the day-to-day marking of written work; this is most effective when it is done with the children so that they can explain clearly how they have approached the task. Insight can be gained into strategies used for arithmetic or how children have approached problem-solving. With the restraints of time this is not always possible, but analysis of marked work will help identify strengths and weaknesses in your teaching as well as the achievements of the children. If there are several children with the same or similar errors, this may reflect the style of teaching you have used. Evaluate and review your teaching methods in order not to perpetuate errors and misconceptions. If the errors are idiosyncratic to individual children these are best dealt with one to one, so that the child can explain how they came to the result.

Short-term assessment does not need formal recording as the action should be immediate. However, it may be useful to keep informal notes on individuals.

Medium-term assessment

The purposes of medium-term assessment are very different from those of short-term assessment. Its focus is to assess what you are not sure about. It is mainly to:

- **review and record the progress children are making over time against key objectives – what they can do and whether they can apply the knowledge and skills learnt to new situations;**
- **assess whether individual targets have been met, including those in Individual Education Plans (IEPs) so that new targets can be set;**
- **provide information for end-of-year assessments and any reporting to parents.**

Your medium-term assessment will help you to identify children's particular strengths and weaknesses. It can also identify trends within your teaching – if one particular area has not been achieved by the majority of the class you should evaluate and assess your teaching. The medium-term assessment should focus on key objectives that you have produced for your half term's work.

Medium-term assessment should influence your next medium-term plans. For example, two days each term should be designated to medium-term assessment and should be planned for groups and individuals. Usually, medium-term assessment takes the form of a written task. It may involve several different ideas and skills linked to one or more of the key objectives. It is good practice to let the children know what is the focus of the assessment: for example, if you are assessing accuracy, you will be looking for workings shown clearly for written calculations, and clear, concise explanations of the methods used to solve problems. Tasks set for medium-term assessment should be chosen so that the children can tackle them independently.

As you assess the work you should have in mind your key objectives, how well these have been achieved and what difficulties remain. Having addressed these points, plan to rectify problems and incorporate your revisions as soon as possible in your next medium-term plans. Written tasks need marking and the children will require constructive written feedback on what they have achieved and how they can improve.

Children's progress needs to be recorded. Records need to be updated about every six weeks and any jotting about an individual child's achievement can aid medium-term assessment. Use a class record of key objectives with a note of the key objectives and a list of the class (see page 35 of the NNS Framework document). Your class record can be dated when you feel that the child has achieved the key objective. You may need some supplementary notes on individual children when their progress towards the key objective is markedly different from the rest of the class. All of this information will need to be passed to the next teacher at the end of the year.

Long-term assessment

This takes place towards the end of the year and children are assessed against school and national targets. It can also be described as summative assessment. Summative assessment is a snapshot of children's learning and achievement at a particular time. It provides evidence of a child's overall learning, usually in the form of a test or a super-vised task. It can take the form of an end-of-topic test or end-of-year test; this can be in the form of the optional QCA tests or end-of-key stage tests.

Summative assessment is useful and necessary but it is not enough — it needs formative assessment to be rigorous, varied and focused to ensure progression (Black and Wiliam, 1999, p.149). Summative assessment is improved by rigorous formative assessment.

The information gained from summative assessment is used in a variety of way. A maths co-ordinator may use it for strategic planning. An area of the mathematics curriculum may show that there is a lack of achievement and progression and the co-ordinator will use this to address the weakness through in-service training for all the staff or for individuals. It may be that the resources for teaching that topic are not appropriate and may need reviewing. The results can be used to give the head an overview or, as in the results of National Tests, the local education authority (LEA) may use them to set targets for individual schools.

Long-term assessment is important in each year group, not just in Year 2 (end of Key Stage 1) and Year 6 (end of Key Stage 2) where the children are compulsorily tested (National Tests — Standard Attainment Targets).

The purposes of long-term assessment are to:

- **assess children's progress against key learning objectives for the year;**
- **assess children's work against national standards at the end of a key stage;**
- **give you supplementary information about children's progress and attainment so that you can report to parents and the next teacher;**
- **help the school set targets for National Curriculum maths tests in future years;**
- **allow head teachers to brief governing bodies, staff and other interested parties on the overall attainment in the school and progress towards school, LEA and national targets.**

The National Tests

Long-term assessment is made mainly through end-of-year tests from Year 2 onwards. There is compulsory testing in Years 2 and 6 and there are supplementary optional test for Years 3, 4 and 5 provided by the QCA. The age-standardised scores help you monitor whether individuals or collectively pupils are attaining results above or below the national average score of 100. It also helps you see progress from year to year, and helps you to use the data to compare with previous years.

Each year the QCA publishes a Standard Report for each key stage, which analyses children's performances in the National Tests. Schools use this information as the starting point to focus on specific aspects of the National Tests and the teaching and learning across the mathematics curriculum and to amend teaching as appropriate. There is also a summary of teachers' assessment usually made against National Curriculum level descriptors and this is usually done in conjunction with colleagues. This process of moderation helps ensure a consistency throughout the school.

Using the National Curriculum and the National Numeracy Strategy

All of the above highlights the importance of assessment in mathematics. Assessing children's progress in mathematics, as in other areas of the curriculum, is multifaceted and involves questioning, discussion, observing, marking and testing and targeting. Making judgements and assessing progression of a child's mathematical understanding, achievements and progress may seem to be a relatively simple process but we need to consider the way in which individuals learn. We can do this by encouraging children to become reflective learners and to get involved in their own target-setting.

In order to help you achieve success in assessment of mathematics we need to address the issues that will face you in assessment. The areas of mathematics in the National Curriculum and the National Numeracy Strategy are as follows:

National Curriculum	National Numeracy Strategy
Key Stage 1	
Number	
Using and applying number	Numbers and the Number System
Numbers and the Number System	Calculations
Calculations	Solving problems
Solving numerical problems	Measures, shape and space
Processing, representing and interpreting data	Handling data
Shape, space and measure	
Using and applying shape, space and measures	

Understanding patterns and properties of shape	
Understanding measures	
Key Stage 2	
Number	
Using and applying number	Numbers and the Number System
Numbers and the Number System	Calculations
Calculations	Solving problems
Solving numerical problems	Measures, shape and space
Shape, space and measures	Handling data
Using and applying shape, space and measures	
Understand properties of shape	
Understanding properties of position of movement	
Understanding measures	
Handling data	
Using and applying handling data	
Processing, representing and interpreting data	

Assessing Using and applying mathematics

There is no mention in the National Numeracy Strategy of the Using and Applying Mathematics strand of the National Curriculum and yet it is an integral part of mathematics teaching and learning and a strand that is used in both key stages of the National Tests.

Practical task

Decide what type of activities could be used in order to assess the Using and Applying mathematics strand accurately, but focus either on Key Stage 1 or 2. Don't try to do the whole of the primary age range as this would be a huge task!

This is a very hard strand to assess. In Key Stage 1 and Key Stage 2 consider whether the children can select the correct operation to solve a problem, select the correct apparatus, talk about what they are doing using the appropriate mathematical vocabulary, and record their findings (informally at first). Can they present results in an organised way and explain their methods and reasoning? The types of activities you may consider in order for children to succeed in this strand are word problems where more than one operation is needed in Key Stage 2. A maths investigation where a number pattern is sought and records have to be kept systematically would again be suitable for children in Key Stage 2. For Key Stage I, you could use a practical measuring lesson and assess whether they can select the appropriate measuring apparatus. Alternatively, from collecting and organising data can they interpret results from the information and present findings in a clear way (also suitable for Key Stage 2)?

Much of the above will require some teaching input, and skills of organising information in a systematic way will need to be developed. Familiarisation with mathematical apparatus will be built up over a period of time. Whilst using and applying mathematics is built into the other strands of the National Curriculum for mathematics it does have its own level descriptors, and you will need to decide which level best fits a child.

ATTAINMENT TARGET I: USING AND APPLYING MATHEMATICS
Teachers should expect attainment at a given level in this attainment target to be demonstrated through activities in which the mathematics from the other attainment targets is at, or very close to, the same level.

Level I
Children use mathematics as an integral part of classroom activities. They represent their work with objects or pictures and discuss it. They recognise and use a simple pattern or relationship.

Level 2
Children select the mathematics they use in some classroom activities. They discuss their work using mathematical language and are beginning to represent it using symbols and simple diagrams. They explain why an answer is correct.

Level 3
Children try different approaches and find ways of overcoming difficulties that arise when they are solving problems. They are beginning to organise their work and check results. Children discuss their mathematics and are beginning to explain their thinking. They use and interpret mathematical symbols and diagrams. Children show that they understand a general statement by finding particular examples that match it.

Level 4
Children are developing their own strategies for solving problems and are using these strategies both in working within mathematics and in applying mathematics to a practical context. They present information and results in a clear and organised way. They search for a solution by trying out their own ideas.

Level 5
In order to carry out tasks and solve mathematical problems, children identify and obtain necessary information. They check their results, considering whether they are sensible. Children show understanding of situations by describing them using symbols, words and diagrams. They draw simple conclusions of their own and give explanations of their reasoning.

Level 6

Children carry out substantial tasks and solve quite complex problems by independently breaking them down into smaller, manageable parts. They interpret, discuss and synthesise information presented in a variety of mathematical forms. Children's writing explains and informs their use of diagrams. Children are beginning to give mathematical justifications.

As stated earlier there has to be a teaching input in order for children to achieve in this strand. However, Burton (1984) believes that:

> *problem solving is only real when pupils take responsibility for their own mathematical thinking.*

This strand above all others helps children develop this type of mathematical autonomy.

You may like to try using the following format for recording children's responses to using and applying mathematics tasks.

Behaviours you are looking for	Yes/no	Evidence	Assessment notes
Identifies clearly what the task is			
Identifies appropriate mathematics skills/knowledge to use with given task			
Works systematically			
Records appropriately			
Identifies appropriate patterns			
Explains results			
Justifies results/conclusions			
Explains patterns/ideas in words, either orally or in writing			
Moves towards appropriate generalised statements about task from specific cases			

Assessing Number

The NNS tells us that:

> an ability to calculate mentally lies at the heart of numeracy. You should emphasise mental
> methods from the Early Years onwards with regular opportunities for all pupils to develop
> the different skills involved.

This is preceded with a variety of examples of skills, knowledge and understanding to
be acquired. Assessment of these would initially fall into short-term assessment.
Emphasis on mental methods is not developed to the exclusion of written methods
but the formal written algorithm, which condenses so many processes, is delayed.

The skill you will need to develop when assessing number is diagnostic assessment. This
not only involves addressing errors and misconceptions; it also involves judging 'readi-
ness' for the next stage of learning. Judging children's accuracy and understanding will
require analysis of errors and misconceptions. Some common errors in number arise
initially with young children not being able to count, not knowing the cardinal value
of a set, or by miscounting or not knowing the order or position of one number in relation to another. Other errors and misconceptions arise in written work when the
child does not understand the algorithm completely. This can be the result of not
completely understanding place value – for example, some pupils see three-digit
numbers as separate digits rather than seeing the number holistically, much in the
same way as we see our telephone numbers or our car registration numbers. Errors
arise when, through not completely understanding the algorithm, a variety of methods
are used in one algorithm. (See Mooney, Briggs, Fletcher and McCullough, 2002, p. 161.)

The National Curriculum for Number has six level descriptors and in order to give a
'best fit' level to a child, evidence has to be collected from a variety of learning situations. Look at the following example from a trainee's consideration of assigning a level
to an individual's work. Notice the type and amount of evidence that has been
collected in order to award the levels given.

In order to award children a National Curriculum level we have to collect a lot of
supporting evidence. The trainee who studied Joshua's number work (pp. 97–99)
decided that he should be awarded a 'best fit' level 3. Her evidence includes number
bonds to 10 and 100, subtracting by using a number line and adding on, expanded written methods for column addition and subtraction, partitioning numbers to help with
addition and solving word problems.

Practical task

*Study the evidence collected by the trainee. With the National Curriculum for
mathematics, try to give Joshua a National Curriculum level.*

Mathematics levels

Ma2 Number and algebra

Joshua

Attainment target 2: number and algebra

Level 1
Pupils count, order, add and subtract numbers when solving problems involving up to 10 objects. They read and write the numbers involved.

Level 2
Pupils count sets of objects reliably, and use mental recall of addition and subtraction facts to 10. They begin to understand the place value of each digit in a number and use this to order numbers up to 100. They choose the appropriate operation when solving addition and subtraction problems. They use the knowledge that subtraction is the inverse of addition. They use mental calculation strategies to solve number problems involving money and measures. They recognise sequences of numbers, including odd and even numbers.

Level 3
Pupils show understanding of place value in numbers up to 1000 and use this to make approximations. They begin to use decimal notation and to recognise negative numbers, in contexts such as money and temperature. Pupils use mental recall of addition and subtraction facts to 20 in solving problems involving larger numbers. They add and subtract numbers with two digits mentally and numbers with three digits using written methods. They use mental recall of the 2, 3, 4, 5 and 10 multiplication tables and derive the associated division facts. They solve whole-number problems involving multiplication or division, including those that give rise to remainders. They use simple fractions that are several parts of a whole and recognise when two simple fractions are equivalent.

Joshua

Key Stage 2 strategies	Y/N	Notes	NC Level
Count on or back in tens or ones or hundreds	yes		
Find a small difference by counting up from the smaller number to largest	Y	count on · on fingers for some	
Count up through the next multiple of 10,100, 1000	✓		
Reorder numbers in calculation			
Add 3/4 small numbers, finding pairs that total 9, 10, 11	✓		
Bridge through a multiple of 10 then adjust	✓	$19 + 21 = 20 + 20$	
Partition into tens and units, adding tens first	✓	- column addition	
Bridge through 100	✓		
Use knowledge of number facts and PV to add/subtract pairs of numbers	✓	used known facts to add pairs	eg 8 +8 = 1
Partition into 5 and a bit when adding 6,7,8, 9			
Add/subtract a near multiple of 10 to or from a two digit number	✓		
Identify near doubles	✓	A lot.	
Use patterns of similar calculations			
Say a subtraction statement corresponding to a given addition statement			
Multiply a number by 10/100 shifting its digits one/two places to the left	✓	V clear.	
Use knowledge of number facts and PV to multiply or divide by 2,5,10, 100			
Use doubling or halving single digits	✓		
Use doubling and halving of two digit numbers	✓	known facts	
Say a division statement corresponding to a given multiplication statement	—	used occasionally	
Use known facts and PV to multiply or divide by 10 and then 100	✓	$10 \times 5 = 50$	
Partition to carry out multiplication	✓		

+/12

white board

*
white board

22 11 ←
mental
oral
test

V clear - when using near doubles. · adjust.

Joshua → level 3 mostly.
  Not all elements achieved

* white board = photocopy taken of whiteboard from mental oral.

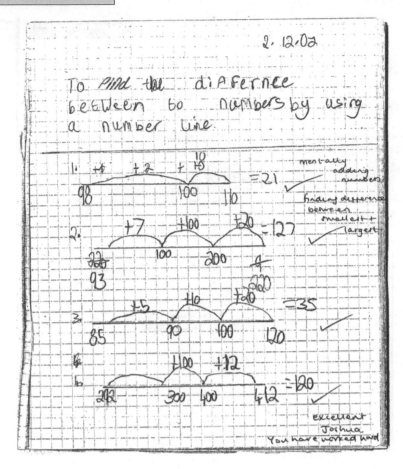

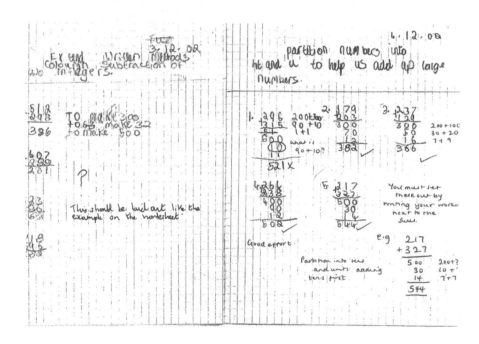

25.11.02

TO solve problems
involving numbers based
on measures.

1. Hull is 200 miles from brighton.
2. plymouth is 218 miles from brighton.
3. There is 110 miles from preston to exter.
4. cambride is 120 miles from brighton.
5. bristol from cambridge from london is 200 miles. 240°
6. The answer would be 373 35 Liverpool, Birmingham, Hull.
7. I could go to Liverpool from preston.

Measurement   Name: JOShua

Numeracy Learning Intention:	Vocabulary:	
To decide which units of measurement would be best to measure different lengths.	Distance	kilometres – km
	Measurement	metres – m
	Units length	millimetres – mm
		centimetres – cm

1. Fill in the gaps by deciding on a situation or an object or the correct unit of measurement.

Situation	Unit of Measurement
Your best friend	m
Clock	cm
all the way round london	Kilometres
A Malteser	m m
Ant	mm
Coventry to London	m
classroom	metres
Home work diary	cm

Excellent.

Challenge:

1. Which piece of measuring equipment would you use to measure:

Table cm   A playing card cm
                                             or mm.

Extension:

Think of some more items or situations that would be measured in cm, mm, km and m. Write them down here with the unit beside it.

Good Joshua.
You have understood
correctly.

There are two aspects of number to assess – oral calculation and written calculations. The following are overviews of the progression of those two areas that could be used as part of the monitoring, assessment and recording process.

Assessing mental/oral number

Key Stage 1 strategies	Y/N	Notes	NC Level
Count on or back in tens or ones (say how far).			
Find a small difference by counting up from the smaller number to largest.			
Reorder numbers in calculation.			
Add 3/4 small numbers by putting largest number first.			
Find pairs that total 9, 10, 11.			
Bridge through a multiple of 10 then adjust.			
Use knowledge of number facts and PV to add/subtract pairs of numbers.			
Partition into 5 and a bit when adding 6, 7, 8, 9.			
Add/subtract a near multiple of 10 to or from a two-digit number.			
Identify near-doubles.			
Use patterns of similar calculations.			
Say a subtraction statement corresponding to a given addition statement.			
Multiply a number by 10/100 shifting its digits one/two places to the left.			
Use knowledge of number facts and PV to multiply or divide by 2, 5, 10, 100.			
Use doubling or halving.			
Say a division statement corresponding to a given multiplication statement.			

Key Stage 2 strategies	Y/N	Notes	NC Level
Count on or back in tens or ones or hundreds.			
Find a small difference by counting up from the smaller number to largest.			
Count up through the next multiple of 10,100, 1000.			
Reorder numbers in calculation.			
Add 3/4 small numbers, finding pairs that total 9, 10, 11.			
Bridge through a multiple of 10 then adjust.			
Partition into tens and units, adding tens first.			
Bridge through 100.			
Use knowledge of number facts and PV to add/subtract pairs of numbers.			
Partition into 5 and a bit when adding 6, 7, 8, 9.			
Add/subtract a near multiple of 10 to or from a two-digit number.			
Identify near-doubles.			
Use patterns of similar calculations.			
Say a subtraction statement corresponding to a given addition statement.			
Multiply a number by 10/100 shifting its digits one/two places to the left.			
Use knowledge of number facts and PV to multiply or divide by 2, 5, 10, 100.			
Use doubling or halving single digits.			
Use doubling and halving of two digit numbers.			
Say a division statement corresponding to a given multiplication statement.			
Use known facts and PV to multiply or divide by 10 and then 100.			
Partition to carry out multiplication.			

Another way of looking at mental maths is to ask children how they do specific calculations to see the strategies they are using. The following is an example of a school-based activity completed by a trainee doing just that with a Year 3 boy called Ben. Here you see the trainee's notes about each calculation that Ben completed.

Ben
(Year 3)

Maths School Based Task

1.   8 + 2 = 10   KNOWN FACT
Because 2 more than 8 is 10.

2.   5 + 5 = 10   KNOWN FACT
I know it

3.   10 + 2 = 12   DERIVED FACT
added 2 and used 2 x table knew that
12 came after 10 in 2x table.

4.   4 + 6 = 10   KNOWN FACT
already know

5.   4 + 7 = 11   DERIVED FACT
                              no.
Just need to add one more to 4.

6.   11 - 2 = 9   COUNTED BACK
Counted back in head

7.   15 - 5 = 10   KNOWN FACT.
I already know.

	Written recording and calculation strategies	Y/N	Notes
Yr1	Record in the context of practical activities and when solving simple number problems, e.g. number sentences.		
Yr2	Develop recording in the context of practical work and explaining how problems were solved, e.g. how much money there would be if there were 5 coins in a box.		
	Use paper and pencil methods to support, record and explain mental addition and subtraction of numbers up to 100, e.g. writing an explanation of how 93 – 89 was calculated mentally.		
Yr3	Use informal paper and pencil methods to support, record and explain mental addition and subtraction of number to 1000, e.g. using an empty number line to show how 301 – 45 was calculated.		
	Begin to use column addition and subtraction, using expanded form, e.g. 456 + 63: 400 + 50 + 6 + 60 + 3 400 + 110 + 9 = 519		
	Explain methods and reasoning, where appropriate, in writing, e.g. explaining how the missing number in a calculation such as 47 + ? = 55 was found.		
Yr4	Develop and refine written methods for column addition and subtraction of two whole numbers less than 1000, and addition of more than two such numbers.		
	Approximate first. Use informal pencil and paper methods to support, record or explain multiplications and divisions.		
	Develop and refine written methods for TUxU and TU/U.		
	Choose and use appropriate ways of calculating (mental, mental with jottings, pencil and paper) to solve problem.		
Yr5	Extend written methods to column addition and subtraction of two integers less than 1000, e.g. 456 + 362		
	Short multiplication of HTU by U.		
	Long multiplication of TU by TU.		
	Short division of HTU by U.		
	Choose and use appropriate ways of calculating (mental, mental with jottings, written methods, calculator).		
	Explain methods and reasoning in writing.		
Yr6	Extend written methods to column addition and subtraction of numbers involving decimals; short multiplication and division of numbers involving decimals; long multiplication of a three-digit by two-digit integer.		
	In solving mathematical problems and problems involving 'real life', explain methods and reasoning in writing.		
	Begin to develop from explaining a generalised relationship in words to expressing it in a formula using letters and symbols.		

The next example shows a trainee's use of evidence provided from recording written calculations completed by Anika, to make judgements about her error and misconceptions. There is a short introduction to Anika to give you initial background information about this pupil.

Anika is a year 1 pupil. She was the probably the most able (in mathematics) out of the low ability group within this particular mixed class. She has English as an Additional Language, this <u>might</u> be related to why she had difficulty identifying words with the same meaning, for example 'add' and 'plus', or it could simply be lack of experience.

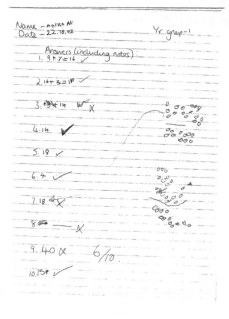

Name – Anika Ali
Date – 22.10.02   Yr group–1

Answers (including notes):
1. 9 + 7 = 16 ✓
2. 16 + 3 = 19 ✓
3. 19 + 14 ✗
4. 14 ✓
5. 19 ✓
6. 4 ✓
7. 18 ✗
8. ✗
9. 40 ✗   6/10
10. 15 ✓

Analysis of Misconceptions and Errors: Anika in Year1.

	Solution strategy	Misconception/ error
Arithmetic task 1: 7 – 3 = Pupil's response: 4	Solution strategy: 'Counting out' Pupil puts up 7 fingers and folds down 3 and knows answer is 4.	Misconception/ error: N/A
Arithmetic task 2: 17 – 11 Pupil's response: 18	Solution strategy: Attempts to 'count out' on paper but cannot apply her strategy due to incorrect pictorial representation of the task - Anika has difficulty visualising problem so tries to represent it using circles on paper. Draws 16 circles instead of 17, then 10 circles instead of 11, and uses a line to separate the minuend and subtrahend; appears unsure of the next step, counts all the numbers, miscounts the circles representing the minuend getting 18, and decides this is her answer.	Misconception/ error: **Defective procedure** – Anika tries to adapt her method from task 1 on to paper and becomes confused in the process, not quite sure of the next step to take. She mistakenly draws out the 10 circles (11) instead of taking this amount away from the 17 (18) circles as she did in her first sum with her fingers. Her intentions were clear at the start but she was not confident with her technique.
Arithmetic task 3: 15 – 6 = Pupil's response: 40 (then crosses out answer). Shying away from writing anything down, still doubting her response to previous task.	Solution strategy: Not clear **It is likely Anika is challenged by the size of the numbers (working across the decade barrier) and would have less trouble working with numbers to ten (within the decade barrier)**	Misconception/ error: **Random response** -pupil does not relate the nature of the problem to the first subtraction problem she solved (7–3=). Her lack of recognition of the nature of the task and the inappropriate size of her answer demonstrates that her understanding of subtraction is not concrete (a sensible guess would have been smaller than the minuend).
Arithmetic task 4: 19 – 12 = Pupil's response: 40	Solution strategy: Not clear	Misconception/ error: **Random response**– Anika makes an instant and random response showing **inconsistent understanding** of subtraction Again, a more suitable guess would be of a number that was smaller than the minuend.
Arithmetic task 5: 20 – 5 = Pupil's response: 15	Solution strategy: 'Counting back from' (it is claimed!) – Anika 'acts out' the process of counting back using her fingers; there is no discernible connection between the numbers she utters and her finger movement – she is imitating a desired technique!	Misconception/ error: N/A Anika claims she counts back and even pretends to count her fingers but I would suggest her answer was a **known fact** due to the speed of her response. She acts out the process of 'counting back from' because she thinks this is what is expected of her (she is taught this strategy in class).

Assessing word problems

A specific difficulty within mathematics assessment is the area of word problems, which are often used to assess whether or not a child can use mathematics in context. You could use a format similar to the one below for recording and assessing children's handling of word problems.

Behaviours you are looking for	Yes/no	Evidence	Assessment notes
Reads the problem			
Can explain what needs to be done			
Chooses appropriate calculation			
Carries out calculation			
Carries out calculation using appropriate accuracy			
Appropriate recording of steps if necessary			
Returns to the problem to check if the answer is reasonable and whether or not units are required			
Explains answer(s) including any necessary rounding			
Justify answer(s)			
Records answer(s) including any units			

ASSESSING MATHEMATICAL LANGUAGE

One area of difficulty for children is the language used in mathematics. One reason for these difficulties is the way everyday language is used in mathematics. For example, if we take the word difference, in everyday language the emphasis is on the visual differences between two or more items, but in mathematics the word is used to describe the numerical difference. If young children are asked what the difference is between 3 and 7, they might say that 3 is curlier, which is accurate but not what you are wanting as an answer. If children do not have a thorough understanding of the language and its precise use in mathematics then they are more likely to misinterpret questions. This may not be because they don't understand the underlying mathematics but they are not clear about the precise use of terms in the mathematical context. Some other specific issues about language in mathematics in different topics are picked up later in this chapter.

Assessing errors, misconceptions and slip-ups in number

Within the confines of this chapter it would be impossible to cover all errors, misconceptions and slip-ups. The first and latter of these are usually straightforward to rectify. Responses such as 'I know what I did wrong now' or 'I forgot to ...' are fairly easy to diagnose and assess during formative assessment. The misconceptions may be harder. Common misconceptions such as the following occur:

- **326 – 117 = 211. Here the child has subtracted the smaller digit from the larger digit and is not seeing the number holistically but as a collection of separate digits.**

- **602 – 437 = 265. Here the child borrowed from the zero but did not decompose the number 602 as 500 + 100 + 2.**

- **542 – 389 = 200. Here the child has reasoned that a larger digit cannot be taken from a smaller one , so herefore it must be a zero.**

(Resnick, 1982, adapted from Brown and Burton, 1978, quoted in Dickson et al ., 1984)

These errors show misconceptions of place value and misunderstanding of the subtraction algorithm. Many misconceptions in algorithms occur because children do not see numbers holistically and because previous generations have not been taught to do so. Many of the recommendations in the National Numeracy Strategy Framework actively encourage teaching that promotes understanding rather than simple recall of facts.

The following is an example from a trainee's school-based task focusing on errors and misconceptions in numeracy. What is reproduced here for you is a sample of Year 4 children's annotated work showing the range of issues arising from the same task.

(1)

(house)

$14 + 12 = 26$ ✓

This sum she knew in her head but I asked her to show her calculation.

```
   14
+  12
  ────
   20  ← 6 + 10
    6  ← 4 + 2 =
  ────
   26
```

$19 + 20 = 39$ ✓

Know it in my head

$36 + 52 = 88$ ✓

```
   36
+  52
  ────
   88
```

she used her fingers to add the numbers together.

$84 + 29 = 111$ ✗

```
+  84
   29
```

$8 + 20 = 100$
$9 + 9 = 11$

This is a very methodical way of adding the numbers together & the way she was taught. However, she added 9 + 4 together incorrectly.

$84 - 12 = 96$

She used her fingers to do this sum. She didn't look at the question carefully & so added the numbers together by counting on.

$43 - 21 = 64$

Again, she didn't look at the question. She added these two numbers in her head.

7. $18 + 4 + 11 - 6 = 39$

$4 + 6 = 10 + 18 = 28 + 11 = 39$

Here I think she found the two numbers that added up to 10 (because this is a lesson I had taught during the week). She again did not look carefully at the process, although if it was all addition she had it correct. However, after she had completed the worksheet I verbally read her this question, pausing at the marked points to allow her a chance to mentally work it out. She got this answer right straight away.

$35 - 18 + 4 - 2 = 18$
$30 - 18 = 2$ I can not understand
$30 - 20$ what she has done here.

$164 + 276 =$

```
   164
+  276
  ────
   440
```
✓

$60 + 76 = 130$

$222 + 291 = 513$ ✓

②

14 + 12 = 26

+14
 12
———
 26 ✓

19 + 20 = 39

+19
 20
———
 39 ✓

36 + 52 = 88

 36
+52
——— ✓
 88

84 + 29 = 113

+84
 29
———
113 ✓

84 (−) 12 = 72   He realised
that the
 −84   process had
  12 ✓   changed to
———   subtraction.
 72

43 − 21 = 22 ✓

 43
−21
———
 22

7. 18 + 4 + 11 − 6 = 30

③23   ①18   ②0x11
+ 7   + 4   − 6
———   +①   ———
 30   ———   7
      23 ✗ had added 8, 4 + 1
to get 13 & did
not then include to
circled '1' in the
164 + 276 = tens column.

 16 4
+ 27 6
——— ✓   Confident when
 4 40   adding no's
together &
clear working
out process.

35 − 18 + 4 − 2 = 22

①235   ②18
=18   + 4
− 2   ———
———   22
 15
has chosen
to add all the
positive no's first.

222 + 291 =

 222
+291
——— ✓
 513

③

$14 + 12 = 2.6$ ✓

$$+\frac{\begin{array}{r}14\\12\end{array}}{26}$$

Good at addition and has a clear method of working out.

$19 + 20 = 3.9$ ✓

$$+\frac{\begin{array}{r}19\\20\end{array}}{3.4}$$

$36 + 52 = 88$ ✓

$$+\frac{\begin{array}{r}36\\52\end{array}}{88}$$

$84 + 29 =$

$$+\frac{\begin{array}{r}84\\29\end{array}}{\cancel{1}13}$$ ✓

$84 - 12 = \cancel{96} \, 72$ ✓

$$-\frac{\begin{array}{r}\cancel{84}\\84\\12\end{array}}{72}$$

added first of all, then realised and corrected himself.

6. $43 - 21 = \cancel{6}64$

$$\ominus\frac{\begin{array}{r}43\\21\end{array}}{64}$$

although he's noticed that the process is subtraction, he has still added the numbers together.

$18 + 4 + 11 - 6 = 27$ ✓

$$+\frac{\begin{array}{r}18\\4\end{array}}{\cancel{22}} \qquad -\frac{\begin{array}{r}+11\\6\end{array}}{22}$$

obviously finds it easier to see the calculation going vertically down the page.

$35 - 18 + 4 - 2 = 26$

$$\begin{array}{r}35\\-18\\+4\\-2\\\hline 26\end{array}$$

9. $164 + 276 =$

$$+\frac{\begin{array}{r}164\\2\,26\end{array}}{441}$$

- calculated this wrongly. otherwise correct.

$222 + 291 =$

$$+\frac{\begin{array}{r}222\\291\end{array}}{513}$$ ✓

(4)

14 + 12 = **26** ✓

$$+\begin{array}{r}14\\12\\\hline .26\end{array}$$

19 + 20 = **39** ✓

$$+\begin{array}{r}19\\20\\\hline 39\end{array}$$

36 + 52 = **88** ✓

$$+\begin{array}{r}36\\52\\\hline 88\end{array}$$

She is good at addition & has a clear method of working out.

84 + 29 = 113 ✓

$$+\begin{array}{r}84\\29\\\hline .11\,3\end{array}$$

84 − 12 = **72**

$$-\begin{array}{r}84\\12\\\hline 72\end{array}$$

She realised that the process had changed to subtraction.

43 − 21 = 2·2 ✓

$$-\begin{array}{r}43\\21\\\hline 2^2\end{array}$$

Here she had the right idea but put the '4' in the wrong place.

8 + 4 + 11 − 6 = **9**

$$\begin{array}{r}18\\+4\\\hline 58\\+11\\\hline 6\,9\end{array}$$

$$\begin{array}{r}^6 9\\-6\\\hline 6\,3\end{array}$$

She worked systematically through her answer — although making a mistake at the beginning, her workings were correct. However she then changed her answer to 9.

35 − 18 + 4 − 2 = **55**

$$-\begin{array}{r}35\\18\\\hline .53\end{array}$$

$$-\begin{array}{r}57\\2\\\hline 55\end{array}$$

She has added the 2 no.s together.

$$+\begin{array}{r}.53\\4\\\hline 57\end{array}$$

She has taken the 5 always from there. ✓

164 + 276 = **440**

$$+\begin{array}{r}164\\276\\\hline .44\,0\end{array}$$ ✓

222 + 291 = **513**

$$+\begin{array}{r}222\\291\\\hline 51\,3\end{array}$$

Errors and misconceptions in the other strands

There are common misconceptions in all areas of mathematics – for example, with measurement, misconceptions can arise with the use of measuring instruments; with time, many misconceptions are connected to the fact that time is not a measurement with base ten. Young children, when learning about money, believe that seven pennies are worth more than a £1 coin simply because there are more of them. Many children, when first coming to school, will have the concepts of certain common shapes but will not have the names for them or know their properties. Diagnosis of errors and misconceptions are essential if planning and teaching are to be effective.

Practical task

Look at the National Tests and the Teacher's Guide for Key Stage 1 and 2 and try to diagnose what sort of misconceptions may occur in the Shape, space and measures strand.

Some of the problems that may arise are problems of sequencing time. The language of time is particularly confusing, with deceptively simple changes such as 9:20 becoming 'twenty past nine', and so reversing the order, creating problems and confusion for children. Another difficulty that arises when teaching time in the classroom is that the children come to it with a variety of home experiences. The connections between analogue and digital displays are conceptually difficult for them. Further, children do not automatically associate the passing of time with a clock; instead, they see it in terms of events – playtime, home time, teatime. Taking this into a weekly, monthly or yearly context gives rise to many of the principal areas for error and misconception. Another area for confusion for children, as mentioned earlier, is that this is the first time they will be working in bases other than base 10. Seconds and minutes operate in base 60; hours and days operate in base 24 and 7 respectively.

With money, one of the problems young children encounter is the difficulty of determining coin recognition and of the value of coins. Their focus is often on the quantity of coins rather than on the value of each item. Generally, children find difficulty in establishing the relationships among the variety of different coins. Money is an area in which many children are experiencing increasing difficulty, as we live in the age of the debit and credit card, and cash is used much less today than in previous generations. For young children, paper money does not have the same appeal as coinage and is therefore dismissed 'as not worth as much'. When using the four operations of number with money they may experience difficulties using the decimal point, which in itself is a decimal notation with a limit of two places for the pence.

The vocabulary relating to space, shape and measure may also cause confusion. Words such as 'pentagon' and 'octagon' can be confused, and thus it is the properties of shapes which should be taught along with the names.

Ainley (1991) has discussed the place of measurement in mathematics and asked the question 'Is there any mathematics in measurement?' Measuring instruments give a range of calibrated scales with a variety of units and unit representations, and the skill of reading scales accurately has to be taught. Children with specific educational needs, such as autistic spectrum disorder, can find the idea of estimating a measurement difficult, as they want to be very precise. Ainley suggests that generally the idea of estimation can cause problems because first, children do not want to be wrong and second, they do not have the life experiences necessary to make estimations with any degree of accuracy. Observing the teaching of measures Ainley says that children do not have sufficient experience of measures in order to make reasonable estimates and that we ask children to estimate too early. This is an important consideration if you are assessing a child's ability to estimate and measure. Children may be trying to be too precise in their estimates as a direct result of being asked to estimate too early, and therefore they have limited measuring experience upon which to base their estimates.

Assessing handling data

Practical task

Look at the progression of Handling data in the NNS and list some areas of possible misconceptions.

Initially children must be able to sort and classify in order to begin to embark on concept acquisition for handling data, and in Key Stage I they must have developed the concept of one-to-one correspondence. Later problems arise for children in the form of labelling axes and of realising the order of Cartesian co-ordinates (the horizontal axis is listed before the vertical axis in the form of $(x,y,)$). Reading the scale off a graph may be problematic and interpreting the findings of the graph may also cause problems.

> The misconception many children have is that the graph is a picture rather than a scale representation. Teachers need to emphasise that each point on the line (in a graph showing the distance a car travelled) represents a distance travelled in a particular time.
> (Mooney, Briggs, Fletcher, and McCullough, 2002, p. 66)

Questioning as an assessment tool

As a result of research carried out by the above team of researchers, there has been more emphasis on formative assessment in the form of effective questioning to enhance learning. The research found that many teachers left too little time for children to respond, often leaving less than one second before posing another question (Rowe, 1974). As a result the only questions that worked were those that relied on rapid recall of known facts, and by their nature were closed questions — for example:

- **What is 5 multiplied by 4?**
- **If I add 22 to a number and get the answer 43, what is my number?**

These closed questions do not take learning forward.

The QCA published a research report in November 2001 entitled *Using assessment to raise achievement in mathematics, Key Stages 1, 2 and 3.* In Section 2 of the report, the use of effective questioning techniques and the merits of using oral questioning as a tool for assessing learning are discussed. In summary, questions are used to assess where the children are in a topic of learning and what they can already do. Questions are used to diagnose specific misconceptions in order to target-teach more effectively.

In order to address the findings in *Working inside the black box* (Black et al, 2002) changes had to be made to questioning techniques. Questions are needed to elicit children's thought processes, attention should be directed at the mathematical language demands made on children, and questions are needed to be asked in order to assess children's current understanding. It has been found that this type of assessment is more effective if the questions asked are open and not closed. For example, 'Tell me some facts that would satisfy a question where the answer is 21' – here the children could display a variety of number facts using one or more number operations; from this the teacher can assess children's current understanding. Often questions are asked that require a recall of facts and are in fact closed questions with one answer – for example, 'What is 5 × 6?' Of course, such questions are necessary to rehearse skills and facts but they do little to promote higher-order thinking skills. Questions that help children to explain their thinking and the strategies they used will develop conceptual understanding. Questions such as 'What do you think you should do next?' or 'Have you seen anything similar to this before?' or 'Can you spot a pattern in what you have done so far?' will promote reflective thoughts that will help develop conceptual understanding.

Assessing the acquisition of knowledge skills and understanding by probing questioning

The NNS has developed 'probing' questions for teachers to use as part of their direct teaching of objectives in the 'Assess and Review' materials (DfES, 2001) in order to:

- **get children to think about the new learning;**
- **make links and so develop a more secure understanding;**
- **explore whether children have any misconceptions, which can be addressed, at the beginning of the main activity;**
- **collect evidence of children's understanding as part of the plenary to inform effective future planning;**
- **identify and rectify errors and misconceptions as part of the plenary.**

An example of probing questions for Year 4 from the materials is as follows:

Key objective: find remainders after division.

- **Do all your divisions have remainders?**
- **Make up some division questions that have a remainder of 1, etc. How did you get your answer?**
- **Make up some division questions that have no remainder. How did you do this? Why won't they have a remainder?**

- **Tell me a number that has no remainder when you divide it by 2, 3 or 5. Are there any others?**

Other examples of appropriate questions are given in *the NNS mathematical vocabulary booklet* (DfEE 1999). These questions are in the form of:

- **What if ...?**
- **How are you going to tackle that ...?**
- **What information have you already got ...?**
- **What question will you need to ask ...?**

A more recent QCA report (2001) has recommended the types of questions that will elicit children's understanding in mathematics:

- **How can we be sure ... ?**
- **What is the same and what is different ... ?**
- **How would you explain ... ?**
- **How do you ... ?**
- **What does that tell us about ... ?**

How do you know if you have chosen the right or inappropriate questions to ask? The following are adapted examples from the same QCA report and show the clear differences between effective and less effective questions for Key Stages 1 and 2. They can also help you to see the differences between the forms of the questions.

Topic	Effective assessment questions	Less effective assessment questions
Calculations	What is the same and what is different about addition and subtraction? Why do 17+9, 18+8 and 19+7 all give the same answer? Why do 5+6 and 6+5 give the same answer? How do you add 9 to another number? Why is it true that 4+4+4+4 is the same as 4×4?	3+? =7 What is 17+9, 18+8 and 19+7? What is 5+6 and 6+5? What is 8+9? What is 4+4+4+4?
Properties of shapes	Why is this picture an example of a shape that has symmetry? How do you explain why the angles in a quadrilateral add up to 360°? Explain the way you have sorted these shapes.	Where are the lines of symmetry on these pictures? What do the angles in this quadrilateral add up to? What shapes have you put in this group?
Properties of triangles	How do you know this is a triangle?	What shape is this?
Fractions and decimals	What is the same and what is different about decimals and fractions?	What is 1/3 as a decimal?
Calculating fractions of quantities	How do you find 1/10 of a number?	What is 1/10 of 36?
Numbers and the number system	What does that tell us about multiples of 9?	Is 47 a multiple of 9?

Practical task

For a specific lesson that you are going to teach, write down some questions that you would ask the children so as to assess their understanding. Check the kind of questions you have formulated against the examples above and make any appropriate changes so they are all effective ones.

Interpreting children's responses to questions

Having used effective questioning as an assessment tool, teachers need to analyse responses and then use this analysis to assess current levels of understanding and misconception. This assessment should then be used to inform planning and to set targets for individuals and/or whole classes.

QCA (2001) shows examples of the responses and how these might be interpreted (the following is adapted from these materials). The table below shows responses to the question put to a group, 'How can we be sure this is a triangle?' The children have been shown a plastic scalene triangle not in horizontal orientation.

Response	Assessment notes
Don't know.	The child may not know the properties of triangles and/or may not be able to identify the properties of the particular shape being held up. Also may not have heard the question.
It's red.	The child is concentrating on visual features of the object and making an incorrect generalisation. (As a teacher you will find it is better to work with clear shapes which focus attention on the properties, rather than drawing attention to other physical features such as size and colour, which are used first by children for sorting activities.)
It's got slanty sides.	The child understands that one property of triangles is related to sides and their orientation towards each other but may not have understood the other properties. (Further questions such as, 'Can you tell me anything else about triangles?' would enable you to find out the extent of the child's knowledge.)
There's three points.	The child understands that one property of triangles is related to the number of vertices but may not have understood the other properties (as above).
It's got three straight sides and three corners.	The child has a generalised concept about the properties of triangles and is able to identify specific cases. (As a teacher you would need to explore this child's understanding of specific vocabulary such as vertices.)

Black et al. (2000) recognised that whilst there are generic strategies which span the range of subjects within the primary curriculum, there some questions which are subject-specific.

In mathematics children have to learn to use valid procedures and to understand the concepts that underpin these. Difficulties can arise when they learn strategies that only apply in a limited context but do not realise that they are inadequate elsewhere. Questioning must then be designed to bring out these strategies for discussion and to explore problems in the understanding of the concept so that the need to change can be grasped. In such learning there is usually a well-defined outcome. In more open exercises, as in investigations of the application of mathematical thinking to everyday problems, there may be a variety of good solutions; then the understanding criteria of quality is harder to achieve and may require an iteration in discussion between examples and the abstract criteria which they exemplify.

Self-assessment

In order for self-assessment to be successful, children must have a clear picture of what is expected of them, the mathematical learning objectives must be explicit, the children must recognise where they are in terms of knowledge, skills and understanding at the beginning of the piece of work and they must know what they are trying to achieve.

Children should be actively involved in setting targets so that they will know what they have to do to bridge the gap between what they know and what they need to know. By taking this sort of responsibility children can become actively involved in their own assessment; in other words, they will recognise when they have achieved. Self-assessment requires children to become reflective as well as critical thinkers. Initially children will need to be guided through this process, as they tend to be self-critical and not recognise their achievements.

In terms of maths self-assessment, the following can be used as part of a structured approach at the end of a topic at Key Stage 2. When this format was used the children became confident and reflective.

Title	
The topic I have covered was ...	
It is in an area/s of mathematics called ...	
In this topic I used my knowledge of ...	1. 2. 3.
I used my skills of ...	1. 2. 3.
The vocabulary of mathematical language that was new to me were the words ...	1. 2. 3. Others were:
I have learnt ...	
I have achieved ...	
I am pleased with ...	
Next time I need to ...	

Self-assessment should be kept as a record either with the topic (however this is recorded), or as a record of achievement for each child. Alternatively, it could be kept in a class 'best work' portfolio.

Self-assessment celebrates achievement and gives the children a sense of ownership of their work. Reflective thought is also achieved by getting the children to set their own targets, which should be realistic and achievable but at the same time should promote challenge. Children need to be aware of when they have achieved success and targets should be regularly reviewed. For Key Stage I one or two key questions could be focused on during a lesson and given to the children, not as a written work-sheet, but orally. Initially no recording of their ideas would be expected but this could be introduced gradually over a number of selected lessons.

Peer assessment

Whist children may be rather self-critical when they first carry out a self-assessment they are less critical of their peers. The purpose of peer assessment is not to rank children but to help children to move forward. Peer assessment needs some teaching input if it is to be successful. When looking at a piece of work the peer assessor needs to consider:

- **Is the work clear?**
- **Is it sensible?**
- **Have all opportunities been explored?**
- **Is it correct?**

Peer assessment is useful as it allows the peer assessor to reflect on his/her own learning and achievements. The QCA document *Using assessment to raise standards in mathematics* (2001) found that:

> Research shows that improving skills in self-assessment and peer assessment is necessary to accomplish other developments essential to effective learning. These include:
> - greater personal responsibility
> - more refection on one's learning
> - enhanced self-esteem and motivation.

Target-setting

Target-setting can be approached in a variety of ways. In some schools targets may be set half-termly, or be set as SMART targets and reviewed on a more frequent basis. They can either be listed in the children's workbooks, or kept in a pocket at the back of the books. Targets are most effective when they are reviewed at regular intervals. They need to have a mathematical content, and not just refer to concentration span, attitudes to behaviour or the amount of work completed.

Effective marking as an assessment tool

Most schools will have a marking policy or at least clear guidelines in relation to the type of marking that is acceptable to a school. Some marking principles are generic but others are specifically applicable to mathematics.

Children should be aware:

- **of what is being marked;**
- **of what is acceptable in terms of clarity of presentation.**

Teachers should:

- **be explicit about what a good piece of mathematics is;**
- **look for success as well as areas that require further development;**
- **make useful comments – if they write 'well done' it should be made explicit why it has been done well;**
- **indicate why work is wrong;**
- **not mark a whole page wrong – the child should be sought out for discussion;**
- **check if targets have been achieved and set new targets, which should be discussed with the child;**
- **take time to talk to particular children if they are unsure of a strategy that is being used;**
- **offer rewards to celebrate success (smiley face, stars, etc.).**

To give you an example of how a teacher might mark a child's work the following is modelled for you.

Abbi   Y3

1.	30 30 $+\ 57$ $50 + 7$ $\overline{77}$ $\dfrac{80\ +\ 7}{87}$	6.	21 $20 + 1$ $-\ 15$ $-10+5$ $\overline{14}$
2.	47 $40 + 7$ $+\ 15$ $\dfrac{10+5}{60+12}$ 52 62	7.	82 $-\ 24$ $\overline{62}$
3.	274 $200+70+4$ $+\ 159$ $100+50+9$ $\overline{323}$	8.	293 $-\ 185$ $\overline{112}$

Abbi, we'll talk about some of these sums.
Can you try number 3 my way – look at
number 1 and 2. Have a go!

You can see the initial comments written by the teacher on Abbi's work but you may find it more helpful to read the teacher's comments and notes to herself below.

Abbi has got so many misconceptions and muddled methods that I have put very few marks on to her work to indicate that whilst I acknowledged them, I realise that an awful lot of work needs to be done with her. The corrections and examples I have done for her are to remind me where I might start with her and try to find out conceptually where she is. I have not written the answer to number 6 as there is decomposition subtraction even after partitioning and I don't think she is ready for that yet. I have asked her to have a go at number 3 on her own as this will give me a starting point for my discussion with her and it will give me a breathing space until I can get to talk to her in the lesson. It will also indicate to me if she can cope with partitioning adding.

Action plan for Abbi

Check place value is secure by partitioning 2/3 digit numbers e.g. 76 = 70 + 6 and 342 = 300 + 40 + 2

Some 2/3 digit addition, no crossing the tens or hundreds by partitioning the numbers as shown.

$$
\begin{array}{r}
36 = 30 + 6 \\
+41 = 40 + 1 \\
\hline
77 \leftarrow 70 + 7
\end{array}
$$

Using the same numbers for subtraction without decomposition:

$$
\begin{array}{r}
77 = 70 + 7 \\
-36 = 30 + 6 \\
\hline
41 \leftarrow 40 + 1
\end{array}
$$

This is as far as I would go at this stage, but I would make a note on my weekly plan for numeracy that when we revisit this objective Abbi has successfully achieved the above and is ready to move on if I have been able to work on these areas individually with her. I would say to Abbi that her work is set out well and shows some good thoughts, look at what I've written, have a go at number 3 after you have looked at numbers 1 and 2. Leave number 6 until I come to talk to you.

My targets for Abbi would be that she is able to add and subtract 2/3 digit numbers crossing 10s and using decomposition but still using partitioning next time the topic is visited.

Practical task

Using the feedback to Abbi as a model, choose a piece of number work from a child you have taught. Mark the work. Consider what comments you will feed back to the child in written form and orally.

The QCA document Using assessment to raise standards in mathematics *(2001) found that:*

Research has shown that pupils who are given only written or spoken comments on how they can improve their work and are not given marks or grades make greater learning gains than pupils given marks or grades only. Those given a combination of marks and comments, which is probably the most widely used form of feedback in our education system make less progress than those given comments only.

You may also wish to consider Butler's study in Israeli schools (1988). She examined the effects of giving one of the following responses to children's work:

* *comments and action for improvement;*
* *grades only;*
* *praise only;*
* *no feedback at all.*

The quality of work of those given comments and action for improvement improved substantially. Those given praise only, or grades only, did no better than those given no feedback at all.

Assessing children using ICT in mathematics lessons

When you assess children using ICT in the mathematics lessons, there a few special considerations of which you need to be aware.

* **Does the program have the same learning objectives as the lesson?**

* **Is the program accessible to all of the children?**

* **Does the program allow for differentiation?**

* **Do the children have the computer skills to operate the program?**

* **Is the focus on the ICT skill rather than the mathematical skills?**

* **How does the use of ICT change the task given?**

* **Does the use of the program enhance the learning?**

* **Does it promote high-order thinking skills?**

* **Is it the best way to learn this piece of mathematics?**

* **If working in pairs or in a group, is there a dominant child?**

The following research summary focuses on how ICT can change the task. In this case, it allows the children opportunities to demonstrate their higher-order thinking skills, which might not be available in a similar task which did not use ICT.

The use of computers as part of the teaching and learning of mathematics can have an impact on the assessment of knowledge, skills and understanding. It is therefore important to be aware of the effect computers can have on learning. This research summary is a specific example of how using the computer with graphs changes the nature of the activity and therefore has a knock-on effect on the assessment outcomes. Pratt (1995) describes the graphing work of children, aged eight and nine years old, who have immediate and continuous access to portable computers across the whole curriculum. The children have used the computers to generate graphs and charts from experimental data. Pratt draws out two distinct uses of the graphing facilities available in spreadsheet software.

1) Passive graphing
Passive graphing is where the children use a graph to display the results at the end of an experiment, and therefore come to see the graph as a presentational tool. The children using this approach made only pseudo-mathematical connections between the graph and the data.

2) Active graphing
Active graphing is where the children use the graphs to help them decide on the next action to be taken in the experiment. They are encouraged to generate the graph after the collection of only a few pieces of data. As they continue to collect data more graphs are drawn and interpretations made. The children are using the graphing as a meaningful and relevant tool.

> **The child who sees graphing as an analytical instrumental has made a powerful mathematical connection which has fundamentally widened that child's grasp of the utility of graphing.**
>
> *(Pratt 1995, p.165)*

Pratt suggests that children encouraged to use the active graphing approach may be in a strong position to make further connections with an algebraic modality. Children who have been using computers to assist them in working in this area may have achieved mathematically more than those who have worked without computers. Therefore the medium used in any assessment would be important in accessing all prior knowledge. That is, assessing without the computer as an aide would potentially give very different outcomes than with the computer. The potential for children achieving higher-order thinking skills with the computer can be seen within the brief summary of the research above.

Record-keeping

Why do we keep records of children's mathematical progress?

- **To chart progression, and use as evidence for the next stage of planning.**
- **To communicate results.**
- **To ensure that there is continuity and no necessary repetition throughout the school.**
- **To ensure there is continuity on transfer to a different phase or school.**
- **To use diagnostically for individuals, groups or whole classes.**
- **To provide information on the success or failure of teaching methods and resources.**

- **To provide information and evidence for interested parties, such as parents, co-ordinators, head teachers, and LEAs.**
- **To allow head teachers to obtain a general picture of progression throughout the school.**
- **For head teachers to have control over the classroom curriculum to ensure each child is receiving equality of entitlement.**

The NNS has produced some class and individual records to help support teachers' recording of assessment. Many schools use year group records at the end of a half-term or term and highlight objectives that most children have achieved in green, those that have caused difficulties in orange, and those that have not been achieved in red. They are able to use these for the next stage of planning. In this way the class teacher and the maths co-ordinator have an overview of achievement, which can also be used as an overview of the effectiveness of the teaching.

There are a variety of blank class records produced commercially or by individual schools. There are some general principles that should apply to all such record-keeping.

- **Lesson learning objectives should be written on the record sheet.**
- **Where a code is used, its translation and purpose should be indicated clearly.**
- **The records should be accessible to interested parties – for example, they could provide a supply teacher with necessary information in order to deliver an effective lesson that ensures progression.**
- **They should be kept up to date.**

NNS-specific intervention after assessment

The NNS has pledged to support the raising of standards for all children. Some children may need support beyond the daily mathematics lesson. As part of the support for teaching and learning mathematics the NNS has developed a range of intervention materials for use in schools. These materials:

- **operate in the context of high-quality teaching during the daily mathematics lesson;**
- **are based on assessment of progression against the key objectives;**
- **are designed to help children who need support to meet age-related expectations against National Curriculum levels and the NNS framework.**

The aims of the programmes are:

- **to set expectations that these children will catch up with their peers;**
- **to support the identified children and to remedy particular difficulties in number so that they are in a better position to access and benefit from the normal teaching programmes in Key Stage 2;**
- **to help teachers and other adults to prepare the additional teaching input to target specific needs;**

- **to help teachers prepare a teaching programme enabling children to benefit fully from the main teaching programme as soon as possible.**

Booster classes

Since the introduction of the NNS there have been several initiatives aimed at improving achievement in mathematics. The first of these, introduced in January 1999, was the creation of booster classes in literacy and numeracy – our attention here will be on the numeracy booster classes only. These classes were designed to give extra, targeted support to children in Year 6. This year group has been without the benefit of the daily mathematics lesson since the beginning of primary schooling. However, booster classes focus on those who are unlikely to achieve level 4 at the end of Key Stage 2 – they are not intended as revision sessions for the whole of Year 6. The majority of schools target small groups of between six and 15 pupils.

In the guidance on organising literacy and numeracy booster classes (2000) it was stated that:

> *Clear learning objective should be determined from the outset followed by a structured programme designed to teach them. Just as pupils have to be carefully targeted, so do elements of English and mathematics that they are taught.*

Using a range of statistical information and evidence from pilot schools the DfEE identified the following to be amongst the topics addressed in booster classes:

- **problem-solving;**
- **how to use a calculator;**
- **fractions, decimals, percentages, ratios and proportion.**

As well as identifying these areas, the NNS team have produced sample Year 6 lessons in a publication called *Sample Year 6 Booster lesson for mathematics* (DfEE, 2000).

Springboard catch-up programme

This programme was first introduced into Year 5 in September 2002. The aim of the programme was to aid children who, without extra help, were unlikely to achieve level 3 in mathematics at the end of Key Stage 2. It has subsequently been introduced to Years 3 and 4. Its main aims are:

- **to support the identified children and to tackle their weaknesses so that they are in a better position to access the numeracy teaching programme relevant to their year;**
- **to set expectations that these children will catch up with their peers and achieve level 4 at the end of Key Stage 2;**
- **to help teachers prepare a teaching programme that enables the children to benefit fully from the main teaching programme for the year relevant to their age.**

The material was designed to be a ten-week, stand-alone course to be delivered to between eight and ten children. The Springboard lessons are in addition to the daily numeracy lessons and consist of a lead lesson, which is teacher-led. A teaching assistant who has attended the lead lesson leads the follow-up sessions. There is published material for each year group by the DfEE. There is also homework material, where the learning objectives are explained to the parent or carer. This shows you how you can target specific groups of children who are underachieving and who need greater consolidation of some of the key objectives in a particular year's programme of work in the NNS.

Further aids to assessment have been produced by the NNS team and published by the DfES:

- *The Assessment Tool Kit to support pupils with English as an additional language (2002).*
- *Supporting more able in Year 5 (2002).*
- *Jottings to support calculations (2003).*
- *Including all children in the literacy hour and daily mathematics lesson (2003).*

Assessment in primary mathematics :
a summary of key points

- *We assess to ensure progression in mathematical learning.*
- *Assessment can be subdivided into short-, medium- and long-term.*
- *Assessment in mathematics must include the correct use of mathematical language as well as a diagnosis of errors and misconceptions in all strands of the curriculum.*
- *Probing questions can be an effective technique for assessing understanding in mathematics.*
- *There is a place for careful self- and peer assessment in mathematics as one of the potential tools for involving children more fully in their own learning.*

Reflection point 4

Having now looked at mathematics this is a good time to stop reading and review.

- *Have your views of assessment in mathematics changed now that you have been involved from the assessor end of the process?*
- *How does your assessment of learners compare with the assessment of yourself as a learner in mathematics?*
- *Have you established clear priorities for an assessment strategy of mathematics?*
- *What subject knowledge might you need in order to be able to identify the potential for errors and misconceptions in the areas of mathematics that you will be teaching?*

Statement	Yes	Not yet	Target	Notes
1. I have a copy of the mathematics subject policy from my placement school or I have notes from reading this document specifically focusing on the assessment section.				
2. I have a copy of the marking policy or I have notes from reading this document specifically related to the teaching and learning of mathematics.				
3. I know what the key objectives for mathematics are that I will be teaching on the next placement.				
4. I have a plan of the assessment strategies I will try during this placement.				
5. I have some formats for record keeping for specific aspects of mathematics that I want to evaluate during this placement.				
6. I have discussed assessment with school-based staff.				
7. I have discussed whether or not there will be opportunities on this placement for being involved in statutory testing in mathematics.				
8. I have seen the records for mathematics of the children I will be teaching.				

4 ASSESSMENT IN PRIMARY SCIENCE

Professional Standards for QTS

 1.3, 2.1, 3.2.1, 3.2.2, 3.2.3, 3.2.4, 3.2.6, 3.2.7

Trainees must demonstrate:

- *that they have secure knowledge and understanding of the science National Curriculum and the framework, methods and expectations set out in the QCA document for science;*
- *their ability to use a range of monitoring and assessment strategies to evaluate children's progress towards planned learning objectives;*
- *their ability to use science assessment information to improve their own planning and teaching and give immediate feedback;*
- *their ability to assess pupils' progress using the relevant science National Curriculum level descriptors;.*
- *their ability to identify and support more able children, and those working below age-related expectations;*
- *their ability to record children's progress and achievement in science systematically to provide evidence of the range of work, progress and attainment over time and use this to help children review their own progress and to inform planning;*
- *their ability to use records as a basis for reporting on pupils' attainment and progress orally and in writing, concisely, informatively and accurately.*

You may find it helpful to read through the appropriate section of the Handbook that accompanies the Standards for the Award of QTS for further clarification and support.

Introduction

Science stimulates and excites pupils' curiosity about phenomena and events in the world around them. It also satisfies this curiosity with knowledge. Because science links direct practical experience with ideas, it can engage learners at many levels. Scientific method is about developing and evaluating explanations through experimental evidence and modelling. This is a spur to critical and creative thought. Through science, pupils understand how major scientific ideas contribute to technological change – impacting on industry, business and medicine and improving quality of life. Pupils recognise the cultural significance of science and trace its worldwide development. They learn to question and discuss science-based issues that may affect their own lives, the direction of society and the future of the world.

(National Curriculum Online, www.nc.uk.net/home.html)

How we view assessment in science depends fundamentally upon our view of what science actually is. Scientists have theories about how the natural and physical world behaves. These theories help them with their explanations and with the need to communicate the theories to others. Often the theories are encapsulated by some form of simple model such as the particulate model of solids, liquids and gases. Scientists constantly seek to test out their theories and models to find out how robust they are in the face of new, experimental evidence, which can be objectively evaluated by others.

As the quotation above suggests, science can be seen as covering two interdependent areas:

- **scientific enquiry;**
- **scientific theories.**

This is reflected in the structure of the National Curriculum for science, where Sc1 covers scientific procedures and Sc2, Sc3 and Sc4 cover scientific theories about living things, materials and physical processes respectively. We will consider this model of science further when we begin to look in more detail at children's learning in science and thus at what we should be assessing in primary science.

You will now be familiar with the general assessment issues that impact on primary classroom practice. You will have noted that what you understand by the term assessment will affect fundamentally the opportunities for assessment you are aware of and act upon in the primary classroom. In order to plan your science lessons with opportunities for assessment in mind, you will need to think carefully about what assessment means. You will also need to understand that the *formative* aspects of assessment are those which are of greatest importance to the interrelationship between planning, teaching and learning.

To be successful, formative assessment needs to collect detailed information about the extent and nature of children's understanding. For example, you will need detailed information about whether children can use aspects of the particulate theory to explain how sugar dissolves in tea. Similarly, you will require detailed information about how children go about testing whether sugar will continue to dissolve in tea and the conditions under which it will dissolve fastest. Such detailed information will give you a clear insight into their scientific understanding, which you can subsequently use in your future planning. This information is fed back into the planning cycle so that you can develop children's ideas in an integrated way in order for the ideas to become more useful and applicable across a wider range of scientific concepts. According to this view of formative assessment, the basis of the assessment process is the continuous, informal observation of children's work in science. This is used to identify what children have achieved, those factors that might be affecting their rate of progress, and thus which teaching strategies will most effectively consolidate and support their future learning. This notion underlies QTS Standard 3.2.1, that teachers:

> *make appropriate use of a range of monitoring and assessment strategies to evaluate pupils' progress towards planned learning objectives, and use this information to improve their own planning and teaching.*

Assessment in science can and should be carried out in a variety of ways. These will range from informal observations, which occur almost as chance events, through to highly structured, formal testing in controlled conditions. It is at the informal end of this spectrum where we will concentrate our attention in this chapter. Any assessment method used to probe children's understanding can only provide us with a partial glimpse of the entire picture. We cannot hope to capture all the knowledge a child has, so we need to use various forms of assessment and to analyse them thoroughly. Unfortunately for the teacher, the various bits of assessment evidence do not always arrive at the same time!

In order to consider assessment in a science context in greater detail we need to examine carefully the following aspects of good primary practice:

- **The meaning of the word assessment and the purpose of assessment.**
- **What to assess, i.e. the assessment criteria you specify in your lesson plan.**
- **How to assess, i.e. the assessment methods you adopt.**
- **The integration of assessment into your planning and teaching.**
- **The records you keep of children's attainment and progress.**
- **How you involve children in self-assessment.**
- **How you identify and measure progression in primary science.**

The meaning and purpose of assessment

We have established that assessment simply means gathering information about a child and comparing it with criteria that relate to the various levels in the development of scientific ideas and skills. The information is gathered through a range of informal methods, some of which involve observing children's actions in the classroom, whilst others use information from the more familiar products of children's work such as their written accounts of practical work. Assessment is absolutely central to teaching and learning. Good teachers are invariably good at assessment and planning with clear learning objectives and assessment in mind. The most important aspect of formative assessment is feedback: this is obtained by gathering and recording assessment information and using that information to plan future activities. The fundamental purpose of continuous assessment by the teacher is to be formative: to inform the teacher's decisions about the types of activities that are likely to lead to improvements in children's learning.

Having established what we mean by assessment and how we might use it to help children make progress in their learning, we can now begin to think about what we will need to assess. Which aspects of children's learning should we focus on in order to help them make progress in science? We can think of children's learning in science located in the following areas:

- **in their knowledge and understanding of scientific concepts (conceptual knowledge);**
- **in their ability to use scientific processes and skills (procedural knowledge);**
- **in their attitudes to science and in their communication skills.**

Knowing what to look for in children's learning in science, and planning activities in sufficient detail to provide the information, are essential elements of effective teaching. They depend on your ability to analyse children's activities in terms of the desired learning outcomes, and on your ability to analyse children's responses. This detailed analysis holds the key to being an effective teacher and to effective assessment. The most productive methods of formative assessment are:

- **finding out children's ideas;**
- **observing children's actions;**
- **listening to children's discussions;**
- **analysing children's written records.**

We consider each of these methods below. At the same time, we need to keep track of the purpose of our assessment activity and the criteria for assessment.

Assessing conceptual knowledge

You will hear a great deal in primary science about children's ideas or concepts. A scientific concept is an idea or network of interconnected ideas used to help explain our observations and experiences of the world around us. For example, we use a concept such as adaptation to help explain and predict the behaviour of plants and animals under different environmental conditions. Similarly we develop concepts of 'energy' and electrical 'current' to help categorise and make sense of a wide range of scientific phenomena and events. Scientific theories are concepts that gain wider acceptance among the scientific community as predictions based on them are borne out by observations and experiments. Extensive research has shown that children form concepts of the world as they experience it, and that these are often at odds with the accepted scientific view. For example, children often believe that the Earth is a saucer-shaped disc, that human beings are not part of the animal kingdom, that plants are not living things because they do not appear to move, or that plants take in 'food' through their roots. They often have little notion of the concept of gravity as a force which pulls objects towards the centre of the Earth.

An important aspect of assessment in science is therefore to establish children's existing ideas and thus their learning needs. A widely used and effective way of identifying ideas is by producing concept maps, discussed and illustrated in earlier chapters. These are representations of relationships between concepts. Concept maps are very useful assessment tools in primary science because they indicate the nature of children's understanding. They are much more than brainstorming activities because children are encouraged to explain and link the words they use. The process of concept mapping can be used with the whole class and is not time-consuming, but it does yield very rich assessment information for teachers to use in their planning. The most effective way to involve children in mapping their own concepts is to provide them with key words written on individual pieces of card. Children are then told to select those words familiar to them and to physically arrange them on a large sheet of paper in a way that makes sense to them. The cards can be moved until the child is content with the arrangement. Lines (or arrows if the children wish) are then drawn between words which they think are related in some way. Single words or short phrases can then be added to explain the nature of the links between words. For young children these explanations can be spoken rather than written. The result of a short mapping exercise may look like this:

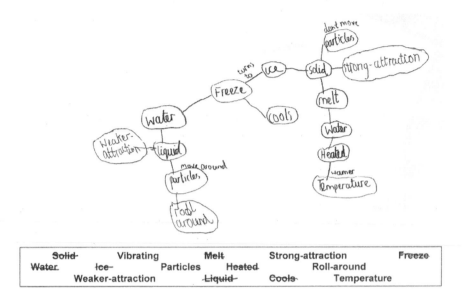

Figure 4.1: Concept map as an assessment aid.

Clearly, these representations are personal and unique to each child. Therefore the teacher can glean from them children's individual learning needs and begin to plan their teaching accordingly. For example, in the concept map shown above, the teacher might wish to explore further the children's understanding of the concept of temperature, cooling, heating and what happens when water in the liquid state is heated further. If concept maps are produced by the children at different stages in the teaching sequence, they reveal to both the teacher and the child what progress is being made and how their ideas are developing as they try to take account of new experiences and the results of their scientific enquiries.

Of course, concept maps are sophisticated representations of children's understandings. For young children this level of sophistication may not be appropriate. The SPACE research project (Liverpool University, 1990) developed alternative methods through which to elicit children's ideas. These included drawings, drawings with explanatory words or notes attached, writing, log books or diaries, and questioning and discussion. The drawings below are a small sample of the types of responses elicited from children. They are taken from the Nuffield Primary Science materials, which were developed directly from the findings of the SPACE research project. They allow us fascinating insights into children's views of the world around them and to their understanding. They provide a rich source of assessment evidence for the teacher in planning the next stages of learning.

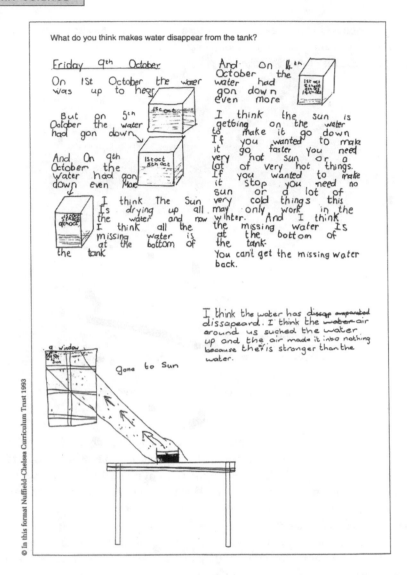

From: Nuffield-Chelsea Curriculum Trust (1993) Nuffield Primary Science S.P.A.C.E. In-service Pack, p. 22.

Figure 4.2: Children's understanding of evaporation.

Scientific skills, which we consider in detail in the next section, can be observed and assessed over a relatively long time-scale, as children are engaged in a wide range of science activities. However, opportunities for assessing children's understanding of concepts may often be much more fleeting and less frequent. It is therefore essential to link children's activities, and thus the opportunities for assessment, to a small number of key ideas. For example, children's ideas about the nature and properties of materials must be assessed through their work on numerous activities, such as testing fabrics for durability, looking at materials used for building, considering how well various materials conduct heat and electricity and how cookery ingredients change when mixed or heated.

One activity in isolation will not provide you with the evidence you need to assess children's understanding of a particular concept. You will need to see not only whether children have understood a concept on one occasion, but also whether or not they can apply that concept to a new situation. For example, having investigated how water freezes, can they use this to predict and explain how butter might behave when it is cooled?

Whilst teaching, you will constantly receive evidence of children's learning. Therefore it is most practical to focus your attention (in assessment terms only!) on a limited number of children in any one lesson. In this way you will be more likely to take notice of significant evidence. Having collected evidence on a number of occasions, you can begin to think in terms of locating children's performance at a particular National Curriculum level. This is by no means an easy task, which is why the Standards suggest that trainee teachers might require guidance from an experienced teacher. We would go a stage further by suggesting that it is essential that you discuss your assessment evidence with experienced colleagues – or probably the science subject leader in your school. In this way you can share the evidence and evaluate and interpret it in relation to the level descriptions of the National Curriculum. Only in this way can you learn how best to identify children's conceptual understanding at a particular level and become more confident in your judgements.

Practical task

During school placement ask to see samples of children's work that has been 'levelled'. Examine these carefully and decide what evidence has been used to match the work to the level descriptions in the science National Curriculum.

Assessing procedural knowledge

How, why and when we use assessment is dependent not only on our view of its meaning and purpose, but also on how we view learning in science. Through the use of process skills, children can learn to examine and restructure their concepts in the light of new evidence from their own enquiries. There is now a vast body of research that suggests that it is much more effective when children do this for themselves than when they are simply led by the teacher. We can now see that the development of procedural and conceptual knowledge is therefore closely interwoven. Children need to engage actively (both physically and mentally) with this process of enquiry. In this way they will have the information they need to modify their existing ideas as they collect new evidence. Clearly, this in turn depends upon children developing attitudes of curiosity, a willingness to work with and listen to the views of others, and flexibility of mind. If you are to provide productive learning experiences, you will need to make continuous judgements about your children based on the observations you make of their performance. We call such judgements assessment, and again you can easily see why it is so important and central to the process of learning.

The effective teacher of science does not simply organise and manage suitable activities in the classroom, providing children with new experiences. If teachers are to address fully the learning requirements of ScI ('Scientific enquiry'), then they must be alert to opportunities to ask and respond to questions. You will need to suggest lines of enquiry if children are to make sense of these new experiences and to learn from them. The process of carrying out scientific enquiries should not be seen as somehow different from or unconnected to conceptual understanding. Scientific process skills play a key role in children's learning. They allow children to use and develop their growing under-standing of ideas and concepts and therefore require specific attention. When planning science activities we therefore need to have in mind both conceptual and procedural learning objectives. Science teaching is both challenging and fascinating because it places considerable responsibility on the teacher. In carrying out the type of formative assessment described above, effective teachers typically engage in ques-tioning and responding to pupils almost constantly. They have a very limited time in which to respond and, during that time, must make judgements about the children's level of understanding and come to an almost instantaneous analysis of how to inter-vene most effectively if they are to help the children make further progress. The teacher must try to arrive at an accurate picture of children's understanding by listen-ing carefully and watching closely as the children go about their work. Children's actions, questions and responses provide important evidence about the way children are thinking and can be fed back into the teacher's short-term interventions and longer-term planning.

ScI is about how children obtain and use evidence from their enquiries to understand the world around them. It involves physical and intellectual skills. These skills can often only be observed as they happen – for example, when children are planning and modifying their investigation as they gather more and more information, perhaps putting forward a number of tentative hypotheses. On every occasion that children take part in some sort of scientific activity they are constantly using procedural knowl-edge and skills. This gives rise to very many opportunities for teachers to assess how well children are using and developing their process skills in a number of different contexts – for example, whether children are using the same skill of observing simila-rities and differences when they are classifying materials on one occasion or types of forces on another. The skill is essentially the same, but the context in which it is used is different. Have the children been able to transfer that skill, or do they need further reinforcement and practice? Every science activity you plan for your children is replete with opportunities for you to add to your evidence and to your picture of children's strengths and areas for further development. Regular focused observations of chil-dren, as they provide evidence of their emerging skills, will enable you to reach a clearer view of their level of attainment and rate of progress.

You may initially be surprised to discover that children apparently operate at different levels when working in different contexts. This highlights the need for continuous assessment on a number of occasions if your picture of children's performance is to be accurate and reliable. Although assessment opportunities are often fleeting and not recorded formally by the children, they are nevertheless significant events which tell us a great deal about their level of understanding. Assessing progress in process skills requires thought and planning. Sometimes it can be inferred from children's writing, drawings and discussions of investigations. More often, the teacher must observe carefully while children carry out their investigations. This does not mean watching intently everything a child does (and worrying about what the others are getting up to!). With good planning, the significant parts of an activity can be identified and observed selectively. For example, you may wish to focus your assessment efforts on children's performance in stating a testable hypothesis on one occasion, on measuring temperature accurately on another, or how well their conclusions fit their results on another.

Practical task

When you next teach a science lesson, decide which enquiry skills from Sc1 you wish to focus on. In your lesson evaluation, describe the children's performance of these skills.

Cavendish et al. (1990, pp. 22–30) suggested that the following process skills are used by children in learning science:

- **observation;**
- **raising questions;**
- **hypothesising;**
- **planning;**
- **measuring;**
- **interpreting data;**
- **recording and communicating;**
- **reflecting critically on procedures.**

We can use these as a procedural checklist when analysing activities in terms of the opportunities they provide for an assessment of children's process skills. Let us now consider one of the units of work (Unit 3D: Rocks and soils) from the QCA Scheme of Work for Key Stages I and 2 as a case study (www.standards.dfee.gov.uk/schemes/science/). We can clearly illustrate how these activities provide us with sufficient scope for observing children. The activities allow us to focus on using observation as an assessment tool as the children set about their practical work and become physically and mentally active. For example, as they:

- **observe and classify rocks in terms of criteria they select and justify;**
- **hypothesise about whether rocks and soils are permeable or easily eroded, in the light of their observations;**
- **devise and plan objective, rigorous tests of, for example, hardness;**
- **think about how best to measure the hardness of rocks or the amount of water which drains through different soils;**
- **think about and try to explain how soil drainage relates to their earlier observations of particle size;**
- **record their results systematically, for example by ranking soils in terms of**

particle size;

- describe and explain their results, for example by demonstrating to their peers with a simple model why water flows through some soil types more readily than others because of the differing particle size;

- discuss those variables they were unable to control and which therefore threaten the validity and reliability of their results – for example, by not repeating measurements of volume of water or time taken or by not measuring these consistently.

Children talking

The thinking of the psychologist L. S. Vygotsky has been influential in science education in recent times. Vygotsky saw that children's experiencies and views of the world around them are formed through the use of language. Children need to communicate their ideas and negotiate meaning through language. He saw that when children talk about what they are doing, they bring their thinking out into the open. They begin to internalise their actions and use this as a basis for planning future actions. That is why children need to communicate their ideas and is the reason why talking to adults and to other children is an integral part of children's learning. We often talk of 'scaffolding' children's activities in order to help them progress beyond their current level of under-standing. The programmes of study for Key Stages 1 and 2 of the National Curriculum for science stress the importance of communication skills in science in the sections headed 'Breadth of study'. They are helpfully linked to the English and mathematics curricula where appropriate.

Key Stage 1:
During the key stage, pupils should be taught to:

Communication
a) *use simple scientific language to communicate ideas and to name and describe living things, materials, phenomena and processes.*

   Links to other subjects: En1 Speaking and listening 1)b
   En1 Speaking and listening 8)c
   En1 Speaking and listening 10)c
   En3 Writing 9)a
   En3 Writing 9)d

Key Stage 2:
During the key stage, pupils should be taught to:

Communication

a) *use appropriate scientific language and terms, including SI units of measurement [for example, metre, newton], to communicate ideas and explain the behaviour of living things, materials, phenomena and processes.*

   Links to other subjects: En1 Speaking and listening 10)a
   En1 Speaking and listening 10)b
   En1 Speaking and listening 10)c

En3 Writing 9)b
En3 Writing 9)c
En3 Writing 9)d
Ma3 Shape, space and measures 1)a

As children talk they are sorting out and organising their ideas. They also learn to modify their own ideas by listening to others. To communicate their findings from scientific enquiries to their peers and teachers, children will have to describe, discuss, interpret and evaluate scientific ideas. This is why talk is so important in providing the teacher with another form of assessment evidence. Listening to children talking is an opportunity both for children to make their own ideas explicit and for the teacher to gather information. It provides an excellent opportunity to assess how well children have understood the activities, how well their science concepts are developing, and how clearly they can communicate ideas. Opportunities for children to present their findings to a wider audience can provide the teacher with insights into children's thinking. A brief session at the end of the lesson led mainly by the teacher does not provide many insights that could be used as part of your assessment strategy. Although science lessons now routinely include a 'plenary' session in the last few minutes of the lesson, there is often insufficient time for children to explore their ideas and understandings thoroughly. Careful planning of this session is required if you are to maximise the opportunities for assessment, link these securely to the lesson objectives, provide children with sufficient time to communicate and explain their findings, and to develop their scientific vocabulary.

Children need plenty of opportunities to demonstrate their learning. The effective teacher of science will keep this in mind throughout the planning and delivery of lessons. These opportunities depend upon the type of role the teacher adopts and the children's response. In science, children often know more than they say. For example, a child might well have controlled certain variables in an experiment or have had a hypothesis in mind, but may not have expressed these things clearly and explicitly. It is therefore part of the teacher's role to encourage children to explain the reasons for their actions. Good science teaching is characterised by activities littered with conversations with individuals and groups of children, aimed at probing their understanding. This approach is firmly grounded in the continuous collection and evaluation of assessment evidence that the teacher subsequently uses to make decisions about the appropriate next stage of learning.

The most effective method for allowing children to demonstrate their growing scientific skills and simultaneously to develop them is through review. Encourage children to spend time and effort critically reviewing their scientific enquiries. Children need time to think through their enquiries at both the planning stage and after the enquiry is complete. Teachers need to listen to and analyse children's thinking in order to assess their understanding. The specific areas for review will include:

- **suggestions for improvements to the method of enquiry;**
- **the accuracy and reliability of the measurements;**
- **the strength of the evidence;**
- **the clarity and accuracy of the recording;**

- explanations of the results and any emerging patterns or trends;
- raising questions for future enquiries.

Several of these areas have also been identified by the QCA in its recent publication, *National curriculum tests 2002 – Implications for teaching and learning from the 2002 tests Key Stage 2 Science*. These can all be planned for and assessed in a well-structured review session. For example, the report states that:

> *teachers can help children improve their performance by:*
> - *expecting them to use the correct technical vocabulary once they have demonstrated they understand a concept*
>   - *... giving them frequent opportunities both to describe what they observe and to explain why things happen ...*
>   - *providing opportunities for them to interpret data, to choose appropriate ways of displaying their results and to explain to others the evidence in the data which supports a particular conclusion*
>   - *making explicit the distinction between 'fair testing' and procedures used to ensure the reliability of results ...*
>   - *providing opportunities for children to ... describe the purpose of a wide range of simple apparatus and measuring instruments ...*
>
> (Source: www.qcashop.org.uk/cgi-bin/qcashop/QCA/02/950.html)

It is often the case that the time taken for exploration, planning and actually carrying out the investigation, precludes the opportunity for review. Teachers often perceive the end point of a scientific enquiry in the primary classroom to be the completion of the practical work and the recording of results. There may also be some brief whole-class discussion and hastily drawn conclusions. Important learning opportunities can be missed in this way. However, detailed assessments of the extent to which children have understood, engaged with, and communicated a scientific approach to their activities can be made if the conditions are right. Significant benefits arise for both teacher and pupils through a planned, structured review session. The National Curriculum programmes of study suggest the structure of such review sessions for ScI under the heading 'Considering evidence and evaluating'.

For example, at Key Stage I:

- make simple comparisons (for example, hand span, shoe size) and identify simple patterns or associations;
- compare what happened with what they expected would happen, and try to explain it, drawing on their knowledge and understanding.
  Links to other subjects: EnI Speaking and listening Ic
                           EnI Speaking and listening 3c
                           En3 Writing Id
                           En3 Writing Ie
- review their work and explain what they did to others.

At Key Stage 2:

- **make comparisons and identify simple patterns or associations in their own observations and measurements or other data.**
  Links to other subjects: Ma2 Number and algebra 2i
  Ma2 Number and algebra4a
  Ma2 Number and algebra 4d
  Ma4 Handling data 2;

- **use observations, measurements or other data to draw conclusions;**

- **decide whether these conclusions agree with any prediction made and/or whether they enable further predictions to be made;**

- **use their scientific knowledge and understanding to explain observations, measurements or other data or conclusions;**

- **review their work and the work of others and describe its significance and limitations.**

Assessing attitudes to science

The introduction to this chapter set out our view of the nature of science and how it should be assessed in the primary classroom. We have seen that science is a striving for understanding. In their search scientists are involved in many activities. For example, they must observe carefully, make notes, check findings, think about possible explanations, read about the work of other scientists, carry out experiments and collect valid and reliable evidence. Obviously, this work requires that those involved in science must think carefully about the strength of their evidence and must have an ability to reflect critically and truthfully on that evidence. Scientists must work methodically, in a way that has been carefully thought out beforehand. Only in this way can they have confidence in their findings and be able to persuade others about their explanations and theories. The scientific activities described above are also all features of good primary science. Although the National Curriculum statements of attainment do not include anything specific about children's attitudes towards science, you will need to assess the extent to which they are developing positive attitudes such as:

- **their level of collaboration and working productively with their peers;**

- **curiosity and the extent to which they are prepared to ask questions and investigate;**

- **whether they are using the required accuracy;**

- **open-mindedness in the light of the views of others;**

- **critical reflection on their work and a willingness to evaluate honestly;**

- **having a respect for evidence rather than seeing what they want to see;**

- **persevering to find alternative ways of solving problems if the initial attempt fails;**

- **their care of living things, the environment and their sense of social responsibility.**

Evidence of children displaying these attitudes can be collected along with the assessment of process skills in a number of different contexts in order to build up a complete picture of the child's performance. In order to encourage the development of these attitudes towards working in a scientific way, the teacher must make an initial assessment, and then monitor progress and decide how best to foster and improve positive attitudes.

Interestingly, these attitudes might also be considered as contributing to the QTS Standards towards which trainee teachers are working. Under the heading 'promoting positive values' (Standard 1.3), those qualifying to teach are required to model such behaviours, values and attitudes so that children learn by example.

Keeping records of children's work in science

Recording children's work is an essential feature of the assessment cycle. It should not be seen as the final product of children's work, but simply as another stage in the cyclical process of planning, teaching and assessing. The primary function of keeping such records is that it will enable you to make sensible, well-informed decisions about the next stage in children's learning. Trainee teachers sometimes become confused and anxious when thinking about how best to keep records of attainment and progress in science. It is important to realise that records are not assessments. However, the methods of recording you choose will reflect the way in which you organise your classroom for science. You may simply decide to take a recording method 'off the shelf', perhaps as suggested in a published scheme of work. However, we believe it is much more important and ultimately more effective if the method you use reflects your approach to learning and embodies those criteria which you have identified to be of greatest value to the children in your class. Whichever method you devise remember that, in order to fulfil a formative role, the record must help to inform your planning and provide a basis for discussion of progress with your pupils and their parents. It should also provide a basis for your own critical self-evaluation of the effectiveness of your teaching.

There is a great deal of variety in the records you will encounter in schools. Checklists or tick sheets are perhaps the most ubiquitous. The least effective and useful of these serves only to record children's experience. Used as the sole means of recording they fulfil little formative function, since they record merely the teacher's subjective judgement about children's performance. The evidence upon which this judgement has been made is missing. Without samples of pupils' work to accompany them, such records are of limited value.

The statements of attainment of the National Curriculum might lead us unwittingly into recording knowledge rather than understanding and skills. For example, it is easy to be persuaded that when a child uses the term 'gravity' he or she understands the concept. This is often not the case, so records must contain evidence of understanding. This should be in the form of teachers' notes to accompany the record or, better still, annotated samples of children's work. Annotations should explain how the teacher came to the judgement that the child had understood. They may be in the form of a written quotation from a child.

When children carry out scientific activities they often produce drawings and diagrams. The graphic standard may not be high, but they often provide evidence of understanding. When accompanied by an explanation by the child (that the teacher may transcribe onto the piece of work in the case of very young children), the graphic becomes much more than a naïve representation; it becomes a powerful assessment device which provides evidence of children's ideas and understandings.

The type of record you choose should be based on your detailed knowledge of the children and your own views about what to assess and the best methods by which to do this. The following is a guide to those things you will need to consider in coming to that decision.

- **Is a simple checklist sufficient to give you evidence that the assessment criteria have been fulfilled by the children?**
- **Does the record provide evidence of children's understanding?**
- **Does it also describe children's difficulties so that the record can be used formatively?**
- **Is your recording procedure sufficiently detailed (for example by using annotations) to allow you to decide upon the most appropriate activities in the next stage of learning?**
- **Does the record give you sufficient information to assess, describe and communicate evidence of attainment and progress to the children themselves, their parents and your colleagues such as the science or assessment co-ordinator?**

Practical task

Collect photocopied samples of children's work. Annotate these to show the children's understanding of concepts or use of enquiry skills.

Your ability to communicate effectively with parents and other interested parties is to a large extent dependent on the rigour and accuracy of your record-keeping. The link between home and school, which may be both formal and informal, is an important aspect of children's primary education. This is particularly true of the core subjects, where such links are relatively obvious and can be exploited for learning opportunities. Those links will be strengthened if the discussions you have with parents are based on a sound and comprehensive recording system. If your record-keeping is rigorous and up to date, parents' consultation evenings are most productive when the teacher can refer directly to specific instances of learning for individual children. Conversations based on this type of assessment evidence will have much greater meaning for parents and carers than simply reporting an attainment level. Indeed, it will help them to contextualise and understand the attainment levels much more easily. If the consultation is backed up by your annotated sample of the children's work drawn from their portfolio, this will prove even more helpful to parents in understanding their child's strengths and areas of learning yet to be developed. We recommend some form of formative assessment record that can be used in the context of specific activities chosen for the learning and assessment opportunities they present. An example of a completed record that would prove very useful for reporting purposes is shown below:

Formative Assessment Record based on close observation

Name: L.T.

Task: To use a model waterwheel (made 'that morning') to raise a weight. (as seen on T.V.)

Possible outcomes	Description	Interpretation	Action
- select and use appropriate materials - select and use appropriate non-standard measures (length and weight) - select and use appropriate units of measure (length and weight)	made about equal contributions with partner. Selected string and a small tub. Cut string too short. I suggested they measure. L. tried handspans rather inappropriate. Watched A. use metre rule. Read it accurately. Listened patiently while partner worked out measure. cm cubes selected as wgts. Counted on in 10's to 100. Suggested they weigh them. Presented with balances and scales. Could use both accurately and was familiar with grams.	Perceived problem well. Can record and interpret length and wgt. cm.　　grams Can use balances and scales Can count in 10's	Further experience on selecting standard v. non standard measures. More challenging problems involving the above

COMMENTS:

From: *Open University (1994) Teaching in Primary Schools Primary Module I Science*, p. 99

Encouraging children's self-assessment

Using formative assessment techniques to improve the effectiveness of your teaching and your pupils' learning by definition presupposes that children themselves have an important role to play in assessment. Children can and should be involved in assessing their own achievements in science. Indeed, QTS Standard 3.2.6 specifically states that before QTS can be awarded trainee teachers:

> must demonstrate that ... they use [assessment evidence] to help pupils review their own progress.

We therefore need to consider ways in which the teacher might encourage this process. Children will not engage with self-assessment naturally but will need help and encouragement, particularly in the early stages. The teacher must first establish a classroom ethos that values the contribution of all the children in the class. The review session mentioned above will provide an important element of the correct ethos. Only when children feel secure and valued will they be prepared to be evaluative and self-critical. They also require very clear criteria against which they can judge their performance. If the teacher were to describe only in general terms how well the class had done a particular activity, the children would have no real picture of their use of scientific concepts and skills. An increasingly apparent feature of the primary classroom is the teacher sharing the lesson objectives and weekly targets with the class. This is easier to achieve in literacy and numeracy than in science, which takes place less frequently. In science, you will come to realise that in order to develop self-assessment skills you must make the criteria for success absolutely clear. Children need to know exactly what was good about their work. Was it the way they attempted to control variables and measure accurately using a thermometer, for example? Or was it the way in which they used their knowledge of sound to predict which material would be best for soundproofing?

The success criteria may come solely from the teacher or be negotiated with individual children or groups. Regular review and target-setting is best achieved when teacher and child meet face to face to discuss progress. This may take only a few minutes but can be very beneficial to both teacher and child. Learning in science improves significantly when teachers and their children have a clear idea about the purpose of a given activity, what they did and understood and what the next step should be. The discussion of success criteria before embarking on an activity increases the children's sense of ownership. Their comments can provide a suitable basis for a progress review and explicit targets for future work can be set. For example, imagine you are about to set your class the task of investigating the effect of the size of a toy parachute on the speed with which it reached the ground. You might then discuss the success criteria with the class: good collaboration within the groups; making sure it was a 'fair test'; using several different sizes of parachutes; measuring their area accurately and using the correct units; accurately timing the descent of the parachute; repeating each measurement; presenting the results clearly in a table; making a clear statement of the main findings.

There are several benefits to be derived from well-planned self-assessment. First and foremost, it encourages children to chart their own progress rather than simply to see their level of attainment in comparison to that of their peers (i.e. norm-referenced). It gives children more responsibility for their own learning; it is motivating for children and reinforces the ethos of teacher and child working together towards common learning goals. A possible framework to encourage self-assessment might take the form of a sentence completion exercise similar to that suggested by Ollerenshaw and Ritchie:

- **The things I enjoyed about the work were …**
- **I discovered that …**
- **I learnt that …**

- I found ... difficult to do because ...
- I think I could improve if ...
- I would like to find out ...
- I don't understand ...
- I know that ...
- I didn't like ...

(Adapted from Ollerenshaw and Ritchie, 1993, p.198)

Communicating and explaining achievement in science is very challenging for both experienced and trainee teachers alike, because the language associated with both its concepts and its procedures is not a part of our everyday vocabulary. For example, we do not routinely talk about 'solubility', 'permeability', 'hypothesising' or 'controlling variables' in our everyday conversations. To help children become better scientists you should endeavour to help them understand such terms in a more general way. The gradual introduction of technical terms in relation to specific activities will familiarise children with the specialised language of science and ensure that there is a common language which will help children understand the criteria for achievement towards which they are working. This is clearly of central importance to any system of self-assessment.

Identifying progression

Progression in children's learning may be defined as a sequence of events or stages that show movement towards a particular educational goal or set of goals. As we have seen, children learning science will show progression on a number of fronts:

- **in their conceptual knowledge (knowledge and understanding of scientific concepts);**
- **in their procedural knowledge (the ability to use scientific processes and skills in appropriate contexts);**
- **in their attitudes towards science and in their social and communication skills.**

The nature and rate of progress is rarely the same for all children. Therefore, the need for accurate, ongoing, formative assessment is self-evident and reinforces the need to include some form of self-assessment as discussed in the previous section. We must try to check understanding, skills and attitudes at frequent intervals in order to monitor the path of each child's progression, and to adjust future work according to our findings. To recognise that progression is taking place some form of assessment is needed. The National Curriculum level descriptions provide us with the criteria against which performance can be judged, so that we can assess whether children have achieved at a particular level. However, the statements of attainment can be regarded as stepping-stones on a journey. They are quite widely spaced and indicate the general direction of travel but are not the actual pathway. Each child's path can be quite different but still lead in the direction of overall progress towards more scientific ideas, skills and attitudes. When children come to a new teacher or a new topic, they will start from different positions. These starting points must be recognised by the teacher in order to help them make their way in the direction of progress. This is not possible without assessing where children begin and constantly monitoring the path they are taking. By doing this you will be fulfilling the requirements for effective teacher assessment.

Assessment in primary science:

a summary of key points

▬▬ *As your assessment skills develop you will feel more and more comfortable probing children's understanding in the same way that you are constantly monitoring children's behaviour.*

▬▬ *Good teaching is all about processing evidence constantly (i.e. assessment). To find out how much a child has understood the teacher must collect evidence and constantly make judgements. This requires analysis and interpretation -- that is, considering the significance of what children say and do. It will entail listening carefully to children's verbal responses; marking children's written work; deciding what feedback is appropriate to the child; annotating examples of pupils' work to indicate when a concept has been grasped or a skill mastered; selecting evidence to keep as a record of achievement; and deciding upon the most appropriate strategy for future activities.*

▬▬ *All this shows us that good assessment is no different whatsoever from the everyday business of the effective primary classroom. Assessment of this type is being carried out constantly. It is very different from standardised, nationally administered tasks and therefore has very different outcomes, but ones which have far greater direct effects on children's learning and on their lasting enjoyment of science.*

The QCA has summed this up well in its description of formative assessment. Central to formative assessment, or 'assessment for learning', is that it:

- *is embedded in the teaching and learning process of which it is an essential part;*
- *shares learning goals with pupils;*
- *helps pupils to know and to recognise the standards to aim for;*
- *provides feedback which leads pupils to identify what they should do next to improve;*
- *has a commitment that every pupil can improve;*
- *involves both teacher and pupils reviewing and reflecting on pupils' performance and progress;*
- *involves pupils in self-assessment.*

(www.qca.org.uk/ca/5-14/afl/summary.sheet.asp)

Reflection point 5

Now you have looked at science assessment in some detail it is time to review your understanding and to identify priorities for any school placement:

- *Have your views of assessment in science changed now that you have reflected on the nature of science, science in the National Curriculum, and your role as teacher as assessor rather than merely teacher as planner?*
- *How does the model of assessment in science set out in this chapter, compare with the way in which you were assessed as a learner in science?*
- *Are you able to set clear learning objectives and identify assessment opportunities within scientific activities?*
- *Are you clear about the role of Sc1 in children's learning and how this can be assessed?*
- *What subject knowledge will you require in order to identify any potential difficulties children could have with the areas of science you will be teaching?*
- *Are you now able to establish clear priorities for your assessment strategy for science?*

Statement	Yes	Not yet	Target	Notes
1. I have a copy of the science subject policy from my placement school or I have notes from reading this document, focusing on the assessment section.				
2. I have a copy of the marking policy or I have notes from reading this document as it relates to the teaching and learning of science.				
3. I know what the key objectives (both procedural and conceptual) are for the science activities I will be teaching on my next placement.				
4. I have a plan of the various assessment strategies I will try out during this placement.				
5. I have some formats for record-keeping for specific aspects of science that I want to evaluate during this placement.				
6. I have discussed science assessment with school-based staff and considered what will go in the portfolio of evidence.				
7. I have discussed whether or not there will be opportunities on this placement for being involved in statutory testing in science.				
8. I have seen the records for science of the children I will be teaching.				
9. I am aware of the likely impact of children's special educational needs on their learning in science.				

5 CONTINUING PROFESSIONAL DEVELOPMENT OF YOUR ASSESSMENT KNOWLEDGE AND SKILLS

Professional Standards for QTS

 1.7

Trainees must demonstrate they are able to improve their own teaching by evaluating it, learning from effective practice of others and from evidence. Trainees are motivated and able to take increasing responsibility for their own professional development.

You may find it helpful to read through the appropriate section of the Handbook that accompanies the Standards for the award of QTS for further clarification and support.

Introduction

This chapter will focus briefly on the potential areas that may be included in your on-going professional development of assessment. It is not intended to cover these areas in detail but to make you aware of the work that is undertaken at school level and in specific roles in school.

Using assessment for school improvement

In order that a school can use assessment information for school improvement, a school needs to ask some questions about current practice in order to establish the starting point for future work:

- **Are there some aspects of the school's work that are more effective than others?**
- **Is it possible to identify why these areas are more effective? What characterises the success of these areas?**
- **When focusing on the outcomes of formal assessment of children, are some groups doing better than others?**
- **Is it possible to identify why there might be differences in achievements?**
- **How do the school's achievements compare with its previous achievements?**
- **How does the school's performance compare with that of others in its benchmarking group and nationally?**
- **Are there any other factors that need to be considered that are not covered elsewhere but have an effect on the performance of the school?**

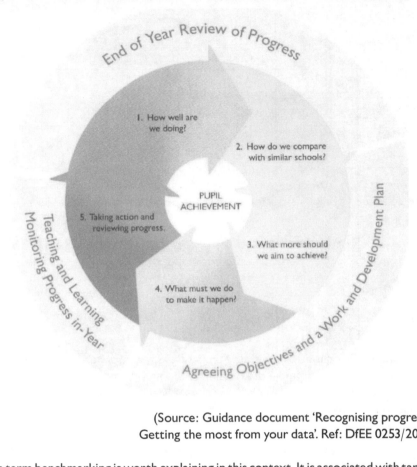

(Source: Guidance document 'Recognising progress – Getting the most from your data'. Ref: DfEE 0253/2000)

The term benchmarking is worth explaining in this context. It is associated with target-setting at school level where schools can compare the performance of groups of similar schools. After comparison, targets are often set for increases in numbers of children to achieve at particular levels. Benchmarking can also be completed for individual children, where they should be in relation to national expectations and what their predicted levels of achievement are. This is much easier to do through the use of data on Assessment manager (discussed briefly later in this chapter).

When looking at assessment results in more detail the questions become more focused:

- **Are the expectations for all children appropriate?**
- **Are there any improvements that can be identified in relation to the school's baseline?**
- **Are there any differences in achievement according to gender?**
- **Are there any differences in achievement according to the class children are in?**
- **Are there differences between subjects?**
- **Are there differences between key stages?**
- **Do the children achieve as well as children in similar schools?**

- **Does the school know what its strengths are?**
- **Is it possible to identify trends in the available data?**
- **Are there any issues arising that surprise the school and its staff?**

From the answers to these questions it is possible to set up an action plan and appropriate target-setting. For more information on the target-setting process at school level, see www.standards.dfes.gov.uk/otherresources/publications/setting/, and for additional information about getting the most from your data see the guidance leaflet already mentioned, reference – DfEE (2000) 0253/2000. The whole process of school improvement is much wider than this, but the other issues are outside the scope of this book.

ASSESSMENT MANAGER

Assessment manager is now part of the Schools Information Management System (SIMS). This is software that allows the tracking of individuals and groups of children within a school and can be updated to show changes. It has been designed to provide the opportunity to record assessment results in computer files and to provide output reports to inform the monitoring processes in a school. Assessment results can be recorded via a keyboard or optical mark reader (OMR) as a mark, a grade or a reading age and these are called the aspect. These are recorded into marksheets with children listed vertically and aspect column codes listed horizontally.

For example, you can create a list of test results as shown on page 148.

The actual spreadsheet looks rather different within the program but this gives you an idea of the process. One difficulty is that all the data must be correct before saving, as you can't delete once the information is saved. From the names and information put in you can create mark sheets that can be printed for use in class. The system will allow you to calculate averages for groups of test results and total scores – these are derived aspects. Grades can be changed into marks to assist calculations. Setting the data range for particular children can create specific reports for individuals, groups or classes.

This is only intended to be a brief outline of the system that is available to schools. Teachers usually attend specific training sessions on precisely how to use these programs in order to use the system effectively. This may be an area that you will become interested in.

Practical task

Find out who is the assessment co-ordinator in school and ask about the computerised record-keeping that is used in school. Find out who uses the inputs and outputs of any system. It may be possible for you to see the information on the system relating to the children you teach. If so, arrange to discuss what the data can tell you about this group with the class teacher or other school-based staff.

Reg: 066P

Name	KS1 Av Pt Score	QCA Y3 Reading Level	QCA Y3 Writing Task	QCA Y3 Maths RS	QCA Y3 Maths Level	QCA Y3 Ment Arit RS	QCA Y4 Reading RS	QCA Y4 Reading Level	QCA Y4 Spelling RS	QCA Y4 Spelling Lev	QCA Y4 Writing Task	QCA Y4 Maths RS	QCA Y4 Maths Level	QCA Y4 Ment Arit RS	QCA Y5 Reading RS	QCA Y5 Reading Level	QCA Y5 Spelling RS	QCA Y5 Spelling Lev	QCA Y5 Writing Task	QCA Y5 Maths RS	QCA Y5 Maths Level	QCA Y5 Ment Arit RS
Anneka (6P)	16	2A	2A	3C	31	2A	7	21	3C	13	3	2C	31	3C	7	19	3A	15	4	22	3A	6
Ali (6P)	21	3C	3C	3C	49	3C	13	21	3C	14	4	3A	49	4	13	25	4C	13	3	37	4C	18
Amy (6P)	21	3C	3C	3C	39	3C	14	31	4	19	4	3A	39	3A	14	30	4B	16	4	42	4C	12
Rhiannon (6P)	21	3B	3B	3B	39	3C	11	34	4	14	3	4	39	3A	11	35	4A	18	5	49	4A	17
Robert (6P)	13																					
Jamie (6P)	21	2C	2C	2C	21	2A	6	22	3B	2	L	2A	21	2A	6	5	L	2	L	28	L	10
Andrew (6P)	19	3A	3A	3C	45	3C	12	27	3A	8	2	2A	45	4	12	23	4C	9	3	46	3B	13
Ian (6P)	21	3B	3B	3B	43	3A	14	29	4	14	3	3A	43	4	14	29	4B	11	3	49	4C	17
Nicholas (6P)	19	3A	3A	3B	45	3A	15	34	4	20	3	3A	45	4	15	35	4A	17	4	52	4B	18
Adam (6P)	19	3A	3A	3B	47	3A	15	26	3A	17	4	3A	47	4	15	28	4B	14	4	49	4A	13
Emily (6P)	17	2A	2A	2B	36	3B	7	25	3B	13	3	2B	36	3B	7	20	3A	11	3	33	3A	9
Abigail (6P)	21	2A	2A	3C	22	2A	6	23	3B	11	3	3B	22	2A	6	23	4C	12	3	27	4C	6
Liam (6P)	15	3B	3B	3A	42	2B	6	26	3A	14	3	3B	42	4	6	38	5	14	4	36	4B	8
Farah (6P)	21	2A	2A	3C	14	2C	2	22	3B	16	3	3B	14	2C	2	23	5	13	3	19	3C	5
Kayleigh (6P)	17	4	4	4	42	3A		28	3A		A	4	42	4		35	4A	17	4	43	4B	8
Adam (6P)	19	3B	3B	2B	33	2A		25	3B	12	3	3C	33	3B	12	29	4B	12	3	28	3A	12
Charlotte (6P)	16	4	4	3B	43	3A	12	37	4	19	4	3A	43	4	10	38	5	15	3	45	4B	14
Luke (6P)	18	3C	3C	2A	35	3A	10	26	3A	12	3	3B	35	3B	5	22	3A	9	3	38	4C	11
Kurtis (6P)	14	2B	2B	2C	26	2B	5	23	3B	11	3	2B	26	2A	8	16	3B	7	L	27	3A	10
Nathan (6P)	14	2C	2C	2C	20	2C	8	21	3C	7	2	2B	20	2B	8	20	3A	3	3	34	3B	10
James (6P)	14	2C	2C	2B	20	2B	11	14	2B	8	3	2B	20	L	11	4	L	6	L	20	3C	9
Simon (6P)	17	3C	3C	2B	35	2A	5	23	3B	4	3	A	35	3B	5	12	3C	8	6	27	3A	11
Emma (6P)	15	3B	3C	3B	40	3B	9	23	3B	10	2	2B	40	3A	9	21	3A	6	3	35	3B	10
Arvinder (6P)	16	3B	3B	2A	36	2A	6	25	3C	13	2	A	36	3C	9	24	4C	12	3	41	4C	14
Amandeep (6P)	15	3B	3B	2C	29	2B	6	19	3C	8	2	2B	29	3C	9	16	3B	7	3	37	3B	14
Fiona (6P)	15	2B	2B	2C	20	2C	6	15	2A	13	3	A	20	2B	6	15	3B	8	3	38	3C	16
Lee (6P)	18	2A	2A	2C	26	2A	8	24	3B	13	3	2C	26	2B	9	16	3B	6	3	27	3B	11
Hayley (6P)	21	3B	3B	3B	35	3C	8	33	4	14	3	2A	35	3B	8	36	4A	11	3	42	4C	14
George (6P)	16	3A	3A	3B	39	3A	8	30	4	13	3	3B	39	3A	8	22	3A	9	3	36	3A	14
Kurt (6P)	19	4	4	3A	45	4	13	35	4	20	4	4	45	4	13	33	4A	18	5	37	4A	16
Rebecca (6P)	16	3C	3C	2B	21	2A	3	26	3A	10	2	2A	21	2A	3	19	3A	19	5	16	3B	4
Emily (6P)	19	3B	3B	3B	34	3B		30	4		A	3A	34	3B		30	4B			30	4C	12
Amy (6P)	14	2C	2C	2C	25	2A	8	22	3B	9	2	2A	25	2A	8	17	3B	6	3	24	3B	10

Co-ordination of assessment as a future role

As part of your continuing professional development (CPD) you will, after your NQT year, be taking on responsibility for subject leadership. The relationship between the Professional Standards for QTS and CPD is shown in a DfES publication entitled 'Teachers' Standards Framework'. This maps the Standards that currently exist and the expectations they contain. The framework summaries the main elements in each of the standards under the ten dimensions of teaching and leadership within a school:

- **knowledge and understanding;**
- **planning and setting expectations;**
- **teaching and managing children's learning;**
- **assessment and evaluation;**
- **children's achievement;**
- **relations with parents and the wider community;**
- **managing own performance and development;**
- **managing and developing staff and other adults;**
- **managing resources;**
- **strategic leadership.**

National Standards for subject leadership

Subject leaders provide professional leadership and management for a subject to secure high-quality teaching, effective use of resources and improved standards of learning and achievement for all children (DfES 2001). These standards are in five parts:

- **Core purpose of the subject leader.**
- **Key outcomes of subject leadership.**
- **Professional knowledge and understanding.**
- **Skills and attributes.**
- **Key areas of subject leadership.**

(TTA, 1998)

Although assessment is not a subject, the co-ordination of assessment practices and data is a key role within any school. Sometimes this is part of the role of the senior management team (SMT), but it may be a role that particularly interests you.

National Tests training

National Tests have not featured as a main focus of the assessment discussed in this book – partly because they are only a small part of the assessment that you will undertake but also because they are subject to change. You will have seen sample questions and may even have tried to answer them yourself – always an interesting experience! You may have been in school at a time when National Tests were being undertaken and so have seen the process in action. If you are teaching a year group or class that includes children who are to take these assessments you will have a wealth of information about how to conduct the assessments and how to mark papers where necessary. You may well be offered opportunities to attend specific training sessions within the school or education authority to support you when you take on this role as a qualified teacher.

Practical task

Find out about what schools and education authorities offer newly qualified teachers to support them with statutory assessments in schools.

Moderation

When National Tests were first introduced there were opportunities to moderate judgements across a group of schools, usually within an authority. As time has passed there are fewer of these opportunities, though you may find that in larger schools teachers still carry out moderation, partly to induct new staff but partly still to reassure themselves about the judgements that they are making.

Practical task

Find out about the moderation that goes on for trainees, NQTs and more experienced staff. Find out what the main focus of these exercises is and see if you can be part of the process.

Continuing professional development :
a summary of key points

- *Assessment will be part of your ongoing professional development.*
- *When working in a school as a qualified teacher you will be more involved with the use of assessment data at school level.*
- *Computerised systems can assist a school in keeping track of children's performance and can be used for school-level target-setting.*
- *You may consider taking on the role of co-ordinating assessment in your school.*
- *In-service sessions will be available as part of your induction and continuing professional development related specifically to National Tests, including the moderation of levels assigned.*

Reflection point 6

Preparing for continuing professional development

Statement	Yes	Not yet	Target for CEP	Notes
1. I have identified clear strengths in the area of assessment.				
2. I have identified clear areas for further development in terms of assessment.				
3. I am confident in assessing children's ICT skills and knowledge within subjects.				
4. I am confident in using ICT to support my assessment and record keeping, e.g. Assessment manager.				
5. I have collected evidence of a range of assessment strategies that I have used on my placements.				
6. I have collected formats for record-keeping to use with a new class as an NQT.				
7. I have discussed assessment and my targets with school-based staff.				
8. I want to develop this area of my practice and become an assessment co-ordinator.				

MARRA: monitoring, assessment, recording, reporting and accountability

Monitoring: the day-to-day monitoring of children's progression; partly completed through evaluations of daily lessons and weekly programmes.

Assessment: the use of a variety of assessment techniques to collect evidence upon which to make judgements about attainment and progress.

Recording: the informal jottings of notes by teachers as they work with children, which can also apply to class and individual records of progress and attainment intended for a wider audience.

Reporting: the process of writing reports for parents and discussing progress and attainment at parent consultations.

Accountability: partly the reporting to parents but also the aggregation of information from testing that is used to produce league tables of schools. The other side of accountability as a teacher is to all the parties involved in the teaching and learning process, the children, the parents and governors. You are accountable for all your actions including the assessment of the children in your class.

Other terms

Achievement: what children have accomplished.

Aggregation: the combining of a child's marks or grades from different assessments to give a single mark or grade. There are often set rules about the weighting of the different sets of marks/grades.

Attainment: what children have accomplished, often linked to the judgement of achievement against National Curriculum levels or key objectives from strategies.

Benchmarking: associated with target-setting at school level where schools can compare performance across a group of similar schools. After comparison, targets are often set for increases in numbers of children to achieve at particular levels.

Brainstorming: the process of collecting ideas about a particular topic that do not have to be connected or evaluated.

Cohort-referenced: referenced against the achievements of the current cohort of children.

Concept: a generalised idea or notion.

Concept-mapping: the process of collecting ideas about a topic that show how the children connect ideas to illustrate their thinking. (See page 128 for more details about this technique.)

Construct-referenced: this is where 'criteria' do not define but exemplify grades; the community of practice shares 'standards' and they are implicit and evolve. (See Wiliam, 1998.)

Content validity: fulfilling the standard by which the assessment matches the teaching programme, and covers the same content areas.

Criterion: the standard against which an assessment might be made usually as a statement of achievement.

Criterion-referenced: assessment referenced against specific criteria. The criteria are predetermined as in the key objectives in the National Literacy and Numeracy strategies. When arguing for a criterion-referenced approach Shipman suggested:

Assessing by judging the strengths and weaknesses of children against a specified standard, or against mastery of skill, or against the ability to apply a method of interpreting information seems natural to teachers. Criterion-referenced assessment is an extension of normal procedures but is also the basis of the remedial actions at the heart of teaching. (Shipman, 1987, p. 7)

Diagnostic: describing an assessment that enables you to find out what a child can do and also where specific difficulties lie in order to plan effectively for the future teaching and learning. It can also be seen as formative though the formative assessment may not give you a specific level of detail about difficulties and whether they are errors or misconceptions. A very useful example of diagnostic assessment is a clinical interview (Ginsburg, 1981). This might sound a daunting challenge for a trainee but what it means in practice is getting a child to do a piece of work and to talk to you while completing the task. You would need to record the dialogue either by taking notes and/or audio recording.

Differentiation: how activities and/or lessons are adapted to meet the diversity of children's needs within a given group.

Evaluation: the judgements made about the effectiveness of activities and or teaching as examples.

Evaluative assessment: assessment outcomes, which are used to see how well teachers or schools are performing.

Face validity: describing either an assessment method looks as though it will allow you to do what it is intended to do.

Formal assessment: this usually refers to assessments that are imposed upon teachers from outside, like National Tests, or other published tests. This type of assessment is usually planned in advance.

Formative assessment: that is completed to inform planning, teaching and learning. It is concerned with the totality of children's knowledge and how their knowledge is integrated and assessed.

Formative recording: recording that may be informal and used as the basis of discussion about target-setting for progress between teacher and child.

Going 'meta': reflecting about your own learning.

Grading: judging a child's work and assigning the work a grade which could be a numerical score (e.g. 9/10) or an alphabetic grade (e.g. a B) or a grade against national curriculum levels (e.g. 3b).

Group assessment: this can be seen in two ways – first, an assessment that is made of a group of children as a whole; and second – as the assessment of individual members of a group based on the group outcomes and individual contributions to any task. The latter is a more difficult task for the teacher than the first.

Informal assessment: this is usually the kind of assessment that a teacher makes while teaching, based upon observations and listening to children's oral responses; it may not be planned in the same way as the formal assessments and therefore is a more integral part of the teaching and learning cycle.

Ipsative: assessment based on past attainment. An example of this would be a portfolio of a child's work in which you could identify progress over time.

Knowledge: what a learner knows and how it can be used.

Learning intentions: an alternative term for learning objective.

Learning objective: a clear statement of what it is intended that children will have learnt during an activity, a lesson or sequence of lessons.

Learning outcome: the actual learning that takes place, not the completed work.

Level descriptions: the specific statements of criteria against which teachers judge levels of achievement according to the levels within the National Curriculum. Each level description describes the kind of skills, knowledge and understanding children working at a particular level should be able to demonstrate. In making decisions about children's levels of attainment, teachers judge which description best fits each particular child.

Manageability: the extent to which assessments can be part of the 'normal' classroom activities.

Marking: judging and making comments upon a child's work, which can include grading.

Metacognition: learning about how to learn.

Moderation: the process of reaching agreement among teachers of assessment outcomes and level of achievements.

National Tests: the term used for the assessments at the end of each Key Stage and the optional materials in Years 3, 4 and 5.

Norm-referenced assessment: assessment that compares the performance of one child against that of other children. An example would be 'sixth in the class'. Most classroom assessment is referenced against the norms of performance of the class as a whole, i.e. what is expected of a specific age group.

Observation: the process of watching children and making notes if appropriate about their behaviours including their learning. (See page 19 for more details about this technique.)

Peer assessment: judgements made by peers about learners' learning.

Performance: a term to describe the observed behaviour of children as they learn.

Portfolio: a collection of children's work collected over time to show the range of progression in a child's learning.

Questioning: using open questions, phrased to encourage children to explore their ideas and reasoning.

Records: the recording of assessment outcomes for future reference.

Record of achievement: a record kept by children of their own progress across the curriculum.

Reliability: the extent to which the assessment outcomes between teachers and assessments are consistent.

Self-assessment: judgements made about learning by the learner.

Self-referencing: involves children in comparing what they have achieved now with what they have achieved previously.

Skill: a specific ability.

Standardised tests: tests based on norm-referenced approaches, meaning that the expected outcomes should produce a 'bell curve' or 'normal distribution' curve.

Subject portfolio: a collection of children's work across age ranges to assist teachers in making judgements about determing levels for children's work within a subject.

Summative: assessment that is completed at the end of a series of lessons on one topic, or at the end of a term, year or key stage. Although the assessment outcomes may be used for target-setting and inform longer-term planning, they give you a picture of a children's attainment at a particular point in time.

Summative recording: a summary record of achievement at a specific point in time.

Target-setting: this can be seen in a number of different ways. First, it can be seen as setting specific learning objectives for individual children. Second, it can describe the same process for a group or class. Finally, it can be seen as setting targets in terms of levels of performance that a school is aiming for over a period of time.

Teacher assessment: assessment of children that is carried out by teachers, which could be in the form of a formative or a summative assessment.

Understanding: demonstrating the use of knowledge and skills.

Validity: the extent to which an assessment measures what it sets out to measure and/or assess.

Ainley, J. (1991) Is there any mathematics in measurement? in Pimm, D. and Love, E. (eds.) *Teaching and learning school mathematics*. London: Hodder and Stoughton.

Askew, M., Brown, M., Johnson, D., Rhodes, V., and Williams, D. (1997) *Raising attainment in numeracy*. Report of a project funded by Nuffield Foundation. London: King's College.

Baroody, A. J. and Bartels, B. (2001) Assessing understanding in mathematics with concept mapping. *Mathematics in Schools*, May 2001, pp. 24–27.

Black, P., Harrison C., Lee C., Marshall B. and Wiliam, D. (2002) *Working inside the black box*. London: King's College.

Black, P. and Wiliam, D. (1998) Assessment and classroom learning. *Assessment in Education*, 5:1.

Black, P. and Wiliam, D. (1998(b)) *Inside the black box: raising achievement through classroom assessment*. London: King's College.

Bristol University (2000) *Don't know what would be a good bit of work, really*. The LEARN Project. Guidance for schools on assessment for learning. Bristol: CLIO Centre for Assessment Studies, University of Bristol.

Brown, G. and Wragg, E.C. (1993) *Questioning*. London: Routledge.

Burton L. (1984) *Thinking things through*. Oxford: Basil Blackwell.

Butler, R. (1988) Enhancing and undermining intrinsic motivation: the effects of tasks involving and ego-involving evaluation on interest and performance. *British Journal of Educational Psychology*. 58:1–14.

Cavendish, S., Galton, M., Hargreaves, L. and Harlen, W. (1990) *Assessing Science in the Primary Classroom: Observing Activities*. London: Paul Chapman.

Christie, F. (1995) Young children's writing: From spoken to written genre, in Bourne, J., Briggs, M., Murphy, P. and Selinger, M. (eds.) *Subject learning in the primary curriculum. Issues in English, science and mathematics*. London: Routledge/The Open University.

Clarke, S. (1998) *Targeting assessment in the primary classroom*. London: Hodder and Stoughton.

Clarke, S. (2001) *Unlocking formative assessment*. London: Hodder and Stoughton.

Clarke, S., Lopez-Charles, G. and McCallum, B. (2001) *Interim report on the first term of the project. Communicating learning intentions, developing success criteria and pupils self-evaluation*. Gillingham 1 Partnership Formative Assessment Project. London: Institute of Education, University of London.

Clarke, S. and McCallum, B. (2001) *Interim report on the second term of the project. Oral feedback and marking against learning intentions*. Gillingham 2 Partnership Formative Assessment Project. London: Institute of Education, University of London.

Clarke, S. and McCallum, B. (2001(b)) *Interim report on the final term of the project. Target setting*. Gillingham 3 Partnership Formative Assessment Project. London: Institute of Education, University of London.

Clemson, D. and Clemson, W. (1991) *The really practical guide to primary assessment*. Cheltenham: Stanley Thornes.

Conner, C. (ed.) (1999) *Assessment in action in the primary school*. London: Falmer Press.

Cooper, B. and Dunne, M. (2000) *Assessing children's mathematical knowledge: Social, class, sex and problem solving*. Buckingham: Open University Press.

DfEE (1999) *The Framework for teaching mathematics from reception to year 6*. London: DfEE.

DfEE (1999) *The National Numeracy Strategy mathematical vocabulary*. London: DfEE.

DfEE (2000) *National Numeracy Strategy: Sample year 6 booster lessons*. London: DfEE.

DfEE (2000) *Grammar for writing*. London: DfEE.

DfEE (2000) *Pupil records and reports*. (Ref:DfEE 0015/2000). London: DfEE.

DfEE (2000) *Recognising progress − Getting the most from your data* (Ref: 0253/2000). London: DfEE.

DfES (1988) *National Curriculum task force for assessment and testing (TFAT): A report*. London: DfES.

DfES (2001) Teachers' standards framework: Helping you to develop. (Issue 1) (Ref: DfES:/0647/2001) available at www.dfes.gov.uk/teachers/professional.development

DfES (2001) *Using assess and review lessons*. London: DfES.

DfES (2002) *National Numeracy Strategy: springboard catch up programmes*. London: DfES.

DfES/TTA (2002) *Qualifying to teach: Professional standards for Qualified Teacher Status and requirements for Initial Teacher Training*. London: DfES.

Evans, N. (2001) Thoughts on assessment and marking. *Primary Science Review*, 68:24−26.

Gipps, C. (1997) *Assessment in primary schools: past, present and future*. London: The British Curriculum Foundation.

Goldsworthy, A. (2000) *Raising attainment in primary science*. Oxford: Ginn/Heinemann.

Goswami, U. (1992) *Analogical reasoning in children*. Hillsdale, New Jersey: Lawrence Erlbaum.

Kempe, A. (1999) Drama in and out of the Literacy Hour. *Literacy Today*, 21. www.literacytrust.org.uk/Pubs/drama.html

Khwaja, C. C. and Saxton, J. (2001) It all depends on the question you ask. *Primary Science Review*, 68:13−14.

Lewis, M. and Wray, D. (1996) *Writing frames: scaffolding children's non-fiction writing*. University of Reading: Reading and Language Information Centre.

Lindsay, C. and Clarke, S. (2001) Enhancing primary science through self- and paired assessment. *Primary Science Review*, 68:15−18.

Liverpool University (1990) *Primary Science Processes and Concept Exploration (SPACE) Reports*. Liverpool: Liverpool University Press.

Medwell, J., Coates, E., Griffiths, V., Minns, H. and Wray, D. (2001) *Primary English: teaching theory and practice*. Exeter: Learning Matters.

Mooney, C., Briggs, M., Fletcher, M. and McCulloch J. (2001) *Primary mathematics: teaching theory and practice*. Exeter: Learning Matters.

Neesom, A. (2000) *Teacher's perceptions of formative assessment*. London: QCA.

OFSTED/DfEE (1996) *Setting targets to raise standards: a survey of good practice*. London: DfEE.

OFSTED (1998) *Secondary education 1994−1997: A review of secondary schools in England*. London: HMSO.

Ollerenshaw, C. and Ritchie, R. (1993) Primary Science – Making it Work. London: David Fulton.

Pratt, D. (1995) Young children's interpretation of experiments mediated through active and passive graphing. *Journal of Computer Assisted Learning*, 11:157–169.

QCA (2000) *The National Curriculum*. London: QCA/DfEE.

QCA (2001) *Using assessment to raise achievement in mathematics in Key Stages 1, 2 and 3*. London: QCA.

QCA (2001) *Implications for teaching and learning*. London: QCA.

QCA (2002) *Assessment for learning*. www.qca.uk/ca/5-14/afl/

QCA (2003) *Changes to assessment 2003*. London: QCA.

Reinke, R.A. (1998) *Challenging the mind, touching the heart: best assessment practices*. Thousand Oaks, CA: Corwin Oaks.

Resnick, L. (1982) (adapted from Brown and Burton, 1978) quoted in Dickson, L., Brown, M. and Gibson, O. (1984) *Children learning maths: a teacher's guide to recent research*. London: Holt, Rinehart and Winston.

Rowe, M.B. (1974) Wait time and rewards as instructional variables: the influences of language, logic and fate control. Part one: wait time. *Journal of Research in Science Teaching*, 11:87–94.

Satterley, D. (1989) *Assessment in schools*. (2nd edition) Oxford: Basil Blackwell.

Shipman, M. (1987) *Assessment in primary and middle schools*. London: Croom Helm.

Wiliam, D. (1998) The validity of teachers' assessments. Paper presented to Working group 6 (Research on the Psychology of Mathematics Teacher Development) of the 22nd annual conference of the International Group for the Psychology of Mathematics Education. Stellenbosch, South Africa, July.

Wragg, E.C. (2001) *Assessment and learning in the primary school*. London: Routledge.

Useful websites

www.ncation.org.uk/subjects

For assistance on determing levels for children's work go to the National Curriculum in Action website, which has separate pages available for maths, English and science for Key Stages 1 and 2. There are also comments about the examples of children's work selected from experienced practitioners to further guide your own judgements.

www.standards.dfes.gov.uk/otherresources/publications/excellence/focus/raising

For information about world-class tests for children between the ages of 9 and 13 this site will be useful and will give further links. This is part of the government's initiative focusing on excellence in the cities.

www.worldclassarena.org/v5/default.htm

This site gives details of available online tests on mathematics and problem-solving and for whom they would be most suitable.

www.nottingham.ac.uk/education/MARS

For information about assessment tasks for mathematics this site will give you information about task trialled by teachers. MARS: mathematics assessment resources service.

www.rba.educ.cam.ac.uk
This site provides information about a DfES-funded research project to raise boys' achievement.

www.qca.org.uk/ca/5-14/afl
See this website for information about articles focusing on assessment for learning, and for links to other assessment sites and issues.

www.thelighthouseforeducation.co.uk/assessment/assessment1.htm
This website provides information about formative assessment in practice in a primary school.

www.assessment-reform-group.org.uk/
For information about the Assessment Reform Group, which has been at the forefront of highlighting the role of assessment in raising standards.

www.stockportmbc.gov.uk/ccm/issue33/assessment.htm
Go to this website for an example of the work in one LEA.

www.cleo.uscm.ac.uk
This site contains useful school-based materials.

www.cse.ucla.edu
This site focuses on America.

atschool.eduweb.co.uk/aaia
For the homepage of the Association of Assessment Inspectors and Advisors.

www.dfee.gov.uk/circulars/dfeepub/mar00
For the circular about changes to children's records and reports.

www.nc.uk/net/
This website provides help on planning teaching and assessing the curriculum for children with learning difficulties and the gifted and talented.

www.ase.org.uk
The website of the Association for Science Education (ASE), which will keep you up to date with current issues. The ASE publication, *Primary Science Review* will be particularly useful to you.

Achieving QTS

The Achieving QTS series includes 20 titles, encompassing *Audit and Test*, *Knowledge and Understanding*, *Teaching Theory and Practice* and *Skills Tests* titles. As well as covering the core primary subject areas, the series addresses issues of teaching and learning across both primary curriculum and secondary phases. The Teacher Training Agency has identified books in this series as high quality resources for trainee teachers. You can find more information on each of these titles on our website: www.learningmatters.co.uk

Assessment for Learning and Teaching in Primary Schools
Mary Briggs, Peter Swatton, Cynthia Martin and Angela Woodfield
176pp ISBN: 1 903300 74 6

Primary English
Audit and Test (second edition)
Doreen Challen
64pp ISBN: 1 903300 86 X

Primary Mathematics
Audit and Test (second edition)
Claire Mooney and Mike Fletcher
52pp ISBN: 1 903300 87 8

Primary Science
Audit and Test (second edition)
John Sharp and Jenny Byrne
80pp ISBN: 1 903300 88 6

Learning and Teaching in Secondary Schools (second edition)
Edited by Viv Ellis
176pp ISBN: 1 84445 004 X

Passing the ICT Skills Test (second edition)
Clive Ferrigan
80pp ISBN: 1 84445 028 7

Passing the Literacy Skills Test
Jim Johnson
80pp ISBN: 1 903300 12 6

Passing the Numeracy Skills Test (third edition)
Mark Patmore
64pp ISBN: 1 903300 94 0

Primary English: Knowledge and Understanding (second edition)
David Wray, Jane Medwell, George Moore and Vivienne Griffiths
224pp ISBN: 1 903300 53 3

Primary English: Teaching Theory and Practice (second edition)
David Wray, Jane Medwell, Hilary Minns, Elizabeth Coates and Vivienne Griffiths
192pp ISBN: 1 903300 54 1

Primary ICT: Knowledge, Understanding and Practice (second edition)
Jane Sharp, Avril Loveless, John Potter and Jonathan Allen
256pp ISBN: 1 903300 59 2

Primary Mathematics: Knowledge and Understanding (second edition)
Claire Mooney, Lindsey Ferrie, Sue Fox, Alice Hansen and Reg Wrathmell
176pp ISBN: 1 903300 55 X

Primary Mathematics: Teaching Theory and Practice (second edition)
Claire Mooney, Mike Fletcher, Mary Briggs and Judith McCullouch
192pp ISBN: 1 903300 56 8

Primary Science: Knowledge and Understanding (second edition)
Rob Johnsey, John Sharp, Graham Peacock and Debbie Wright
232pp ISBN: 1 903300 57 6

Primary Science: Teaching Theory and Practice (second edition)
John Sharp, Graham Peacock, Rob Johnsey, Shirley Simon and Robin Smith
140pp ISBN: 1 903300 58 4

Professional Studies: Primary Phase (second edition)
Kate Jacques and Rob Hyland
224pp ISBN: 1 903300 60 6

Teaching Arts in Primary Schools
Stephanie Penny, Susan Young, Raywen Ford and Lawry Price
192pp ISBN: 1 903300 35 5

Teaching Citizenship in Primary Schools
Hilary Claire
160pp ISBN: 1 84445 010 4

Teaching Foundation Stage
Edited by Iris Keating
200pp ISBN: 1 903300 33 9

Teaching Humanities in Primary Schools
Pat Hoodless, Sue Bermingham, Elaine McCreery and Paul Bowen
192pp ISBN: 1 903300 36 3

To order please phone our order line 0845 230 9000 or send an official order or cheque to
BEBC, Albion Close, Parkstone, Poole, BH12 3LL
Order online at www.learningmatters.co.uk